GodPorn

Finding Faith in Netflix, Dave Chapelle, Brené Brown, Jimi Hendrix, the Book of Satan, Bill Gates, Kanye West, the Rolling Stones, Kobe Bryant, Heavenly Cocaine, Michael Jordan, TED Talks, the Beatles, Mr. Rogers, Tom Waits, Muhammad Ali, Stephen Colbert, and Other Stuff.

MIKE LYON

GodPorn—Finding Faith in Netflix, Dave Chapelle, Brené Brown, Jimi Hendrix, the Book of Satan, Bill Gates, Kanye West, the Rolling Stones, Kobe Bryant, Heavenly Cocaine, Michael Jordan, TED Talks, the Beatles, Mr. Rogers, Tom Waits, Muhammad Ali, Stephen Colbert, and Other Stuff.
© 2020 by Mike Lyon

Artistic Lyon
3200 Main St, Unit #3.2
Dallas, TX 75226
www.artisticlyon.com

Printed in the United States of America
First Printing in 2020
ISBN: 978-1-7329974-1-7

Library of Congress Control Number: 2020923990

CONTENTS

FREE DOWNLOAD

Sign up for the Artistic Lyon mailing list, and receive two
Free chapters from #1 bestseller *I'm Not Hitler*. In 2021
you'll also receive two
FREE chapters from GodPorn 2.
Click here to get started: www/artisticlyon.com/FREE

INTRODUCTION

Our western culture pummels us with around-the-clock content. Information comes fast and furious, some is total shite, much of it of the highest caliber. It makes for a funnel ready to burst, and we can drown as we fight to distinguish what's eternal from a waddle in the kiddie pool.

I'm grateful to God for giving me the words to deposit on these pages. I hope the following vignettes provoke thought and help your days be inspired in some way. Much of this content is selfish in origin; but it helps me fight through each day. You may feel of similar ilk, where many days are a battle to make it to the evening, where I can pour a bourbon and turn on Netflix. Sure, lots of escapism and numbing-out happening—no argument. But I don't think I'm an anomaly. Certain days, weeks, and months are filled with battle fatigue, and numbing is the best option available.

I hope you find my 52-week attempt to connect faith with art, film, music, and politics, to be a beneficial journey of exploring how our Lord manifests in culture. In my experience, one of the most difficult leaps to make is seeing how the God of the Bible is relevant in twenty-first-century America. May the contents of this book be a roapmap to the Lord. I pray the Holy Spirit filters accordingly, where only God's words and purposes shine through to your heart.

WEEK 1

TICK-TOCK-TICK-TOCK-BUH-BYE

"The one thing I know for sure about China is, I will never know China. It's too big, too old, too diverse, too deep. There's simply not enough time."

—*Anthony Bourdain*[1]

I remember when I heard Anthony Bourdain utter that line with his distinctive baritone voice. You could hear the resignation, the realization that no matter how hard you live large with purposeful agency, no one escapes the ticking clock. Bourdain did laps around the world. Most of us only dare to live vicariously through people like him, not ever genuinely living out our own purpose. Hell, most of us run from even *asking* about purpose, let alone owning it. Even if we do step out on the plank and risk a smidgen of our heart, we run out of time, or the brief moments of captured validity slip away like a fish on a dock. Tick-tock-tick-tock . . .

There's a powerful scripture that helps narrow our focus between fluffy cotton candy and the meat of life.

> Yet you do not know what your life will be like tomorrow. You are just a vapor that appears for a little while and then vanishes away (James 4:14 NASB).

What do we do with that verse? It can cause sheer panic if we don't think beyond the moment. In other words, we become near-sighted and attempt to live out a series of bucket lists, striving for experiential living. Sure, go for it. I do too. Tasting life through work, travel, food, and culture is crucial to the bigger puzzle. But consider if you derive deep fulfillment from those commodities. Do you? Sure, for fleeting moments.

In my first book, *I'm Not Hitler*, I mention watching the biopic *Quincy* and being astounded by Quincy Jones's prodigious output. Watch the film and then try to name anyone who's come close to his career. Pick any industry. Picasso? Steve Jobs? Beethoven? I couldn't find anyone with that kind of longevity and breadth—couldn't pinpoint anyone who jumped genres and combined composition, production, and personal artistry like he did (he was a highly regarded trumpeter). Jones's career is the equivalent of Tom Brady winning a Super Bowl in five different decades. Not a chance that would happen for any player in any sport. However, in the film, Jones touches on a deep-seated fear of either running from something or desperately chasing a demon to prove himself. Even if I rationalize and think *Wow. He crushed it. Bravo to a life well-lived*, that's *HIS* life, not mine. What do I do with my own ticking clock?

Tick-tock-tick-tock, and adios, we're gone. I remember being eighteen years old and thinking when I reached twenty-five, I would have life discerned and ordered, with a shiny Porsche validating my transformation from idiot-boy to seasoned man of the world. Yep, that was a spit-take you heard, me chortling at the lunacy I recognize now.

The deeper I go into scripture, combined with how often life takes my knees out, I realize how the brevity of my years forces me to chisel away the bullshit and strive for impact. Not career impact, not fame, not traveling to every country for a selfie. The only thing that matters in the end will be obedience to the Lord, which must result in sacrificial service to people. The stuff that will resonate in the next life will be the times we helped our children learn to ride their bikes AND tenaciously pursue a relationship with God. It will be the times we said, "You were right and I was wrong. I apologize." It will be the moments we sacrificed our almighty agendas and skipped the client lunch and instead took time to look someone in the eye at Austin Street Center and say, "Nice to meet you, Sir/Ma'am. What's your name?"

Tick-tock-tick-tock . . . Lord, help me use Your time well.

Explore:

1) Do you live with a sense of urgency for the important things in life? How do you trust which items are worthy of focus?

2) Is it difficult for you to be obedient to the Lord? What kinds of things keep you from serving God's people well?

Week 2

THE BULLSHIT OF BRENÉ BROWN

"People can be at their most vulnerable, but still tenacious at the same time."

—*Toni Bernhard*[2]

There's an art to cussing. When used correctly, a well placed *bullshit* or *fuck* really brings a story home. Brené Brown has polished this skillset to doctorate-level mastery.

In her new Netflix special, she continues ownership of her space as the purveyor of vulnerability. If you're not familiar with her work, her books *Daring Greatly* and *The Gifts of Imperfection* are desert-island musts. She gets to the heart of living with her key tenet: vulnerability is where true courage begins. Our culture says the opposite: armor up, don't show weakness, go for the throat. One of the many takeaways in this nearly comedic special is her riff on failure. Not being *open* to failing, but actual failure. I'm talking about failing where you don't know the next option, where the safety net for the safety net is gone, where you finally realize how little control you genuinely have.

In a similarly excellent read, *Emotionally Healthy Spirituality,* Peter Scazerro references Saint John of the Cross's poem "Dark Night of the Soul." The thesis of the poem is what he calls the joyful experience of being steered to God. The only light in this dark night is the one that burns in the soul and leads us to God. In other words, it's being taken to the mat when all the platitudes in the world can't pick you up. It's the place where you think our loving God has turned against you. That's the vulnerability Brené is talking about. It's where real life begins because it's scary as fuck to be completely surrendered to the results (which if you're a man or woman in the arena, will be bad). Some outcomes must include failure . . . major failure. If not, you haven't risked beyond your means of scrappiness. I've failed with five businesses and lost over $1.2 million of investor capital. I planned, we followed best practices, my teams executed. The net result? Abject failure, where you wonder if your brain is pickled and your future is nothing more than recapping "what the fuck happened?" I've questioned past decisions, which made me scared to make the next ones. Ahh, but that means I'm stepping out of Teddy Roosevelt's arena. That's taking a seat in the stands with the tepid souls with clean shirts and no scar tissue. As Brené reminds us, staying in the arena requires continuous openness to being kicked again with no chance of success.

But there is victory in the recognition of your tribe. When you meet someone of the same ilk, there's a connection of knowing you're from the same platoon. There's a knowing smile and slight nod, a fist bump of confirmation that you bled and became real.

Explore:

1) Have you failed big? Have you been taken to the mat with no clue how to stand up again?
2) Are you willing to step into the arena and fight the big battles even if the outcome might include failure?

WEEK 3

THE MASKS WE WEAR

"He who is most deeply abased and alarmed, by the consciousness of his disgrace, nakedness, want, and misery, has made the greatest progress in the knowledge of himself."

—*John Calvin*[3]

I have an ongoing mime-esque gesture I do with friends and acquaintances where I pretend to grab the bottom of my chin and pull my hand back over my head, as if removing a mask. Hilarity and applause ensue as I bow to the multitudes.

The reality is, we are all wearing masks as we perform, pretend, and, on some occasions, live our adulthood. Think about how often we put on our "game face" as we do dinner with the boss or spend time with the in-laws on a holiday. As much as we'd like to speak our minds to the proverbial kooky uncle spouting conspiracy theories, we smile and nod as we wish for a cyanide pill to end the agony.

While watching the Netflix miniseries *Killer Inside: The Mind of Aaron Hernandez*, I found myself asking how many masks I wear and how deep my façade is. There are plenty of opinions on Hernandez's tragic story, and the *Salon* article about the miniseries is one of many negative reviews. *Salon*'s perspective, like many others, questioned the focus of the content. For me, I found myself defaulting back to the swirling thoughts and personalities we try to camouflage.

Viewed through a spiritual lens, I kept thinking about families of origin and the wounds we try to numb or erase from our memories. If the series is correct, Hernandez had a litany of struggles: his own sexuality, a hair-trigger temper, and sociopathic tendencies.

There's a temptation to think *That dude's crazy*, followed by *I would never do something so deranged*. I used to say similar things. Then the more I understood my own brokenness—an awareness that only comes from knowing Christ—the more I became aware of my depravity, the Bible's word for our stunning moral corruption. Why do I say a person needs Christ to understand how fucked up they are? Because of the ever-present masks. Without insight from the Supreme Being who created us, we'll lie to ourselves about our relative goodness. We need an outside source to shine a light on the deep crevices where we hide like roaches waiting to scamper. Here's an easy measure: how often do we read stories about crimes of passion? People can enact extreme emotional and physical pain on those they love deeply. How is this possible? Depravity stemming from an incurable cancer, eradicated only through the grace of Christ.

One of my favorite pastors, Tim Keller, wrote a line about King David of the Old Testament that I've tattooed on my brain. David sent his top soldier and friend, Uriah, to die in battle to cover up his affair with Uriah's wife, Bathsheba. Check out 2 Samuel 11 for the narrative. Keller says (paraphrasing), "As soon as you say you would never do what David did (pause for effect) . . . you've taken your first step toward doing that act." He brilliantly captures the episode here:

> He [David] covets the man's wife, he commits adultery with the man's wife, he murders the man, and then he lies to cover it up, half the Ten Commandments being broken in one awful enterprise.

Keller goes on to say these chilling words in the same sermon:

> Here's what it teaches us. The seeds of the most terrible possible atrocities, the capability of the worst possible deeds, live in every human heart, even the best people, even people who are converted by God. Whoever you are, even the best people who have ever lived are capable of this. The seeds of those things, the seeds of the worst possible deeds are right now in your heart. That's the teaching.[4]

That's the enlightenment in the Hernandez series. The parts that I couldn't shake from my memory were the home security videos of Hernandez cheerfully playing with his infant daughter with his buddies the morning after they had executed a friend. That's where scripture becomes such a powerful reminder of our hearts. King David is also the man who wrote many of our most inspiring psalms, including Psalm 40:8: "I delight to do your will, O my God; your law is within my heart" (NASB).

I find tremendous joy in pursuing a life of service, prayer, and surrender to Christ. Like David, I know the difference between right and wrong because God's law and grace have been written on my heart. I also know the fragility of the boundaries stopping me from the same trespasses of King David and Aaron Hernandez.

Explore:

1) Are you living your life without hiding behind a mask or masks?
2) Do you trust your own instincts over the Bible? How do you know when you're right or wrong?

WEEK 4

BOW DOWN TO THE JOKER

"If people knew how hard I had to work to gain my mastery
it would not seem so wonderful at all."

—*attributed to Michelangelo*

I'll die happy if I never hear "Abracadabra" or "Rock'n Me" again. In fact, I can't hit the thumbs-down button fast enough on Spotify or Pandora when I hear 90% of classic rock. But my-my-hey-hey, how a fella can get a pertinent kick in the teeth and have their perspective changed.

In the fantastic *Texas Monthly* article "Growing Up with Steve Miller," we get to peer inside the mind of a scrappy creative who combines right brain artistry with left brain, steel-toed operations. This insight, for example:

> If I wanted to "climb the mountain," he told me
> I'd need a routine. I'd need to master my song-
> writing voice: writing every day, charting other

songs' chord progressions, feeling out the rhythms of words and the arcs of melodies. I'd need to tighten up my guitar voice: practicing scales every day, exploring tone in my fingers and through an amp. I'd need to find my singing voice: practicing scales, studying harmony, controlling my breath, learning to shape tones in my throat and phrase them through a line. I'd also need to find the right musicians, practice until we were a single organism, and figure out how to bring a song to life in a crappy venue with a bad P.A. Of course, we'd also need to develop an aesthetic and learn how to produce. Then, if we pulled all that off, we'd need to set up a publishing company and sign a contract that preserved our blood in an industry famous for leeches. After that, I'd really have to get to work.[5]

That, my friends, is the attitude of a startup "mapmaker," to use my preferred word. Some folks follow a map; others draw their own. Steve Miller rolled up his sleeves and ground it out. Much of the quote above is applicable to any organization: exploring tone, creating culture, practicing until the team becomes a singular focused organism staying on message. All endeavors require unbridled tenacity for any level of luck to occur. In other words, luck doesn't find the fortunate. It finds the sweaty, bloody souls who shut themselves away and work. And yes, the favor of the Lord is a must as He sprinkles grace dust as protein.

The Steve Miller Band visits forty to fifty cities each tour. The back-of-the-napkin math looks like this:

40 cities x 5000 fans each show x $50 min ticket =
$10M gross for 90 days of work

30 yrs of tours x $10M gross =

A $300M FU to my snobby attitude regarding classic rock
That FU comes as he puffs Cuban cigars while splitting time between the San Juan Islands in Washington and a home near the ski village of Sun Valley, Idaho. You go, ya big Space Cowboy. Thank you for the humbling reminder of what professionalism looks like.

I've had several people ask me how I wrote my first book. I relied on lessons from Julia Cameron's classic *The Artist's Way*. She says to write for fifteen minutes or write three pages. Every. Day! Even if you repeat "I have nothing to say" over and over until the timer dings. I wrote for an hour a day Monday through Friday from early October until Thanksgiving of that year. Some days the words flowed, but plenty of other days I shook my head with disgust as I plinked out "Me no how write good . . . dammit!"

And so it is. Every project, painting, or business I've begun has included slogging through the fear, the inevitable suck, the doubt of *finishability*. Expect it, don't hide from it, lean in, and produce output.

Explore:

1) Are you urgent about creating a map to follow with the Lord leading the way, whether good or bad?
2) Is fear a driver that propels you forward, or do you shy away from taking risks due to fear?

WEEK 5

WHAT'S MY NAME?

"There is zero chance of being a good person without doing good for others!"

—*Mehmet Murat ildan*[6]

Many of us recall the iconic scene from AMC's *Breaking Bad* when Walter White demands his drug rival say his name: "Heisenberg." A fantastic vignette in television history.

Nothing against Bryan Cranston, but he had as many takes as he needed to nail the scene. Plus, the rival was an actor reading his lines. Not exactly a mystery as to the outcome. Muhammad Ali challenged a rival the same way in a live event, in the center of a ring, in front of thousands of fans. On February 7, 1967, Ali fought Ernie Terrell in the Houston Astrodome. In the two-part HBO series *What's My Name: Muhammad Ali*, you see Ali as he beat Terrell savagely during the bout, but never moved in for the knockout. Throughout the fight, Ali asked Terrell, "What's my name?" due to Terrell's refusal to acknowledge Ali's name change from Cassius Clay in a pre-fight press conference. Ali's sheer ferocity is chilling as you see and hear him demand retribution as he literally beats the man into submitting to his will.

The documentary is a reminder of how gargantuan a character Ali was during the sixties and seventies. We forget that Ali performed at the highest level while under suffocating scrutiny from the American white public, the national media, and members of his own race. Imagine if, in 2019, Lebron James converted to Islam and went to court to avoid fighting in a U.S. war. The response would have been deafening, I can't imagine the fortitude it required for Ali to stand up for what he believed in and still dominate in the ring. He wasn't participating in a team sport where other players could carry the load. His sport is mano-a-mano. Keep in mind this was a time when Martin Luther King Jr., Malcolm X, and Bobby Kennedy were all assassinated, almost entirely due to their rightful stance on African-American civil rights.

The thing about that film and Ali that keeps me up at night is Ali's firm belief that God was using him as an instrument for righteousness. He was. Ali inspired people throughout his life to fight for what's right, that all men are equal and deserving of their seat at every table, whether political, economic, or the neighbor next door. Amen to that. The challenge is this, and it's touched on briefly when Ali meets with Martin Luther King Jr.—Islam and Christianity have fundamentally different foundational doctrines. Islam says Christ was a prophet; Christianity says He's the Savior of the world, the only Son of God, and part of the Trinity. As much as we wish that these two major faiths could both be right, they can't be due to the law of contradictory truths. Either one is right or both are wrong, but they can't both be right. It's like saying a person is dead *and* alive. In our current culture of pluralism, this ain't a popular idea. Plenty of folks live by the idea that "your truth is yours and mine is mine." But that concept has challenges for another day . . . as in, how do we know which person has the right truth? For clarity, I'm not questioning Ali's stance on equality. 100% alignment.

Here's what scares me. Let's say God *does* evaluate entry to heaven based on merit—in other words, based on a person's good deeds. Lots of people have that belief. If that's the case, I'm in a bit of a pickle compared to Muhammad Ali. He impacted and inspired millions of lives and donated millions of dollars to charity. If God measures our lives based on cultural impact, I'm way down the list compared to Ali. Sure, there's a chance God might say, "No worries, just impact the lives around you." Fair enough, but how do I find out exactly what He's measuring in terms of impact? I've donated money to charities, but is there a required lifetime amount? Or what if there's a certain number of times I have to volunteer to offset all the times I've been jealous, snarky, or selfish? Uh, gulp . . . I really don't like this line of questioning.

I have friends who get pissed off when I walk this trail. They default to a position of "Look, man, I just do my best!" and rest in an ambiguous position without definitive metrics. Let me ask it this way: please tell me the perfect list of what's required for me to enter heaven when I die. Yes, I understand I must love my neighbor, but I don't always. Hell, I don't always *like* my own friends. I realize I need to be selfless and do my best to not hurt others, but I haven't been doing the former and have been doing the latter. This is where that Jesus dude becomes a grace-filled alternative. Go read up on Him.

Explore:

1) Do you have a definitive measure of good deeds to ensure God will allow you into heaven? Where did you find the list—or did you create it yourself? Is it authoritative?

2) Muhammad Ali impacted the world. If you were measured against him or Mother Teresa, or even a physician who has saved lives, could you rationalize with the Lord to have Him lower the bar for you to be good enough for heaven?

WEEK 6

CONS, HIV & THE ENEMY
FOR ALL OF US

*"Half of the harm that is done in this world is due to people
who want to feel important."*

—*T.S. Eliot*

Nathaniel Penn's gut-punch 2019 piece for *GQ* is titled "The
Curious Cons of the Man Who Wouldn't Die." It's riveting and
has moments of despair, sadness, and shake-your-head frustration
at the hurt and desperation in this world.

Our incessant need to prove ourselves at all costs comes to
mind . . . or sibling rivalry, or how we set our sights on succeeding
in an industry, or the boundaries between hope, wishful thinking,
and outright fraud. The story is tragic; it reminds of the AIDS
epidemic of the late eighties and early nineties, which hits close
to home for me. My first cousin died at twenty-eight from the
disease. He was a year older than me at the time, and it was not

a peaceful passing by any stretch of the imagination. Like Luke Olmsted in the *GQ* story, my cousin was not promiscuous, and his life was cut short. It's so easy and disgraceful to point fingers and say that his same-sex preference was the cause. Hmm . . . well, what about my hetero lifestyle and cavalier recklessness with my promiscuity? It's never a one-to-one, binary outcome when we're looking down our noses. Life ain't fair, and countless people don't get what we feel they deserve. Most of us live like fallen angels, if we're honest.

With Memorial Day providing a brief moment to reflect, I got to thinking about mankind's history of war in relation to Olmsted's internal, biological battle. No century or people group escapes military escalation. The U.S. has had several large-scale wars: the Revolutionary War, the War of 1812, several wars against Native American tribes, the Mexican-American War, the Civil War, the Spanish-American War, World War I, World War II, the Korean War, the Vietnam War, the Gulf War, and the Iraq War. Those are only ours. Pick pretty much any country, and they have their own litany. The Troubles between Northern Ireland and the Republic of Ireland from the late 1960s to the Good Friday Agreement of 1998. The seventy-year fight between Israel and Palestine, which biblical scholars claim stems from real estate discussed in the Old Testament books of Genesis, Leviticus, and Deuteronomy. That's simply the tip of the spear with the Middle East. As a friend of mine said over the weekend while discussing HBO's amazing new miniseries *Chernobyl*, "What is wrong with us!?" Yessir, we do like us some fighting and control of the narrative, don't we?

In the *GQ* piece, we read about Mark Olmsted's ongoing struggles with his T cell count, the common killer of people with HIV and AIDS. "HIV progresses by invading and destroying the body's T cells, which fight infection."[7] That got me thinking: at our deepest core, at a DNA level, there are "invasions" occurring. There's always an enemy to refute. Why is that? How many small battles do you fight every day? Not just traffic or your team, boss, clients, kids, and spouse. Everything about our life is a battle. Do we stop and think why, at every level, there's a war raging? Think of movies: whether it's a rom com, a Western, or science fiction, we have good and evil battling. The Outlaw Josey Wales seeks justice; Luke Skywalker battles with the dark side of the Force manifested in Darth Vader. Sound like baloney in real life? How about the battle to count calories? The fight to get out of bed each morning? The constant onslaught of anxiety and fear?

Galatians 5:17 perfectly captures this onslaught, as scripture so often does.

> For the flesh desires what is contrary to the Spirit, and the Spirit what is contrary to the flesh. They are in conflict with each other, so that you are not to do whatever you want.

I'm fascinated at how blindly I march through life at times, not realizing the havoc raging internally. All those teeny little frustrations that lead to headache and fatigue; all the life events not going as I hoped. Our modern culture doesn't like the word "sin," but that's what Galatians and the entirety of scripture speaks about. Let's call it "mistakes" instead—a more palatable word. All of our mistakes—from the small frustrations of life to committing fraud in order to keep dreams alive all the way up to full-scale war— yes, they all stem from the original mistakes of Adam and Eve. Uh, whuh!? Yes; any problem you find in this world stems from a massive fracture that originated in Genesis chapters 2 through 4. Read it and wrestle with it. Find and study the writings of scholars who unwrap the meaning. Process what Romans 8:22 means when it says "For we know that the whole creation groans and suffers the pains of childbirth together until now" (NASB). That conflict rages in every cell of every person in every country. Nope, not a con. This is truth.

Explore:

1) Are you aware of the internal battles in your mind? Do you attribute them to a spiritual enemy or a secular issue?
2) Is it possible for humankind to truly get along? If God is not the answer, what is?

WEEK 7

MY. NAME. IS. ROBOT.

*"I met an old lady once, almost one hundred years old, and
she told me, 'There are only two questions that human beings
have ever fought over, all through history. How much do you
love me? And Who's in charge?'"*

—*Elizabeth Gilbert,* Eat, Pray, Love[8]

A friend and I got into an interesting discussion about HBO's
miniseries *Chernobyl.* The score and music are extraordinary, literally an additional character carrying the story; the sound effects
seem to speak their own lines, creating a powerful current flowing
throughout. My one teeny gripe: I'm not crazy about foreign dra-
mas not being acted in their native language. I don't mind subtitles
at all; I'm a nerd like that. However, hearing British actors call each
other "comrade" is stultifying. But I'm splitting hairs.

What hits you square in the eye is the power of men and governments as they control lives. In this case, it's the Soviet government (under Mikhail Gorbachev) that had not fully exercised its

policy of glasnost. There was very much an iron grip of socialism; the state was always right, and people sacrificed truth for what was best for the state, no matter the consequence. The KGB had its eyes on everyone, and in a fantastic scene, the head of the KGB points to people who are even following him.

This led me to think, *how much leash does the Lord give us? Does He want us to pursue nuclear energy, or is that a Pandora's Box too far above our pay grade? Has our hubris overruled our need for safety?* This tangent led to whether fire is equally dangerous. It certainly has proven benefits for warmth and cooking, but at what point does a valuable thing become a dangerous thing we should never have messed with in the first place?

Now, before we go and beat up on those evil Russian baddies, are we really any different in our robotic pursuit of capitalistic value? As soon as I dogpile on socialist states, I better toss hand grenades at the shortcuts I'll take and backs I'll stab to achieve my dreams of wealth and influence in our free will economy. Yes, at the end of the day, as Winston Churchill said, "No one pretends that democracy is perfect or all-wise. Indeed it has been said that democracy is the worst form of Government except for all those other forms that have been tried from time to time."[9]

I agree. But I did pause during my two humanitarian aid trips to Cuba in the last fifteen years. There, the locals told me they don't agree with their Communist government, but they also had no understanding of homelessness and abject poverty because those things don't exist there.

Chernobyl seems like a good segue to a timeless devotional I read, *My Utmost for His Highest* by Oswald Chambers. Be warned: the great and mighty Oz, as my friends and I call him, is a theological ass-kick. Bring some bandages to this party, cuz your NOSE.

WILL. BLEED. Like this little warm and fuzzy gem from the May 30th entry:

> Jesus Christ demands the same unrestrained, adventurous spirit in those who have placed their trust in Him that the natural man exhibits. If a person is ever going to do anything worthwhile, there will be times when he must risk everything by his leap in the dark. In the spiritual realm, Jesus Christ demands that you risk everything you hold on to or believe through common sense, and leap by faith into what He says.[10]

That's a consistent theme with the great and mighty Oz—who, by the way, probably had two or three giant mastiffs he kept full by feeding them cute little Totos as snacks. Oswald often speaks of common sense as the enemy of our state of mind. He goes against the grain of our modern American culture by pushing hard against the idea of staying in our robotic, capitalistic lane. Oswald lands on the theologically accurate side of the fence that says to abandon yourself to a faith-driven life led by God. I can unequivocally guarantee that this path will not include any mention of retirement or a 401(k) plan. It will, however, lead to a boundary-removed life that, in hindsight, will be a one-hundred-times bigger adventure than you could ever dream. Why? Because you don't have the mental faculties to dream as big a life as God can for you. Try this an exercise: dream as big as you can dream. Where do you land? Be honest. Probably a beautiful spouse; tall, athletic, Mensa-member kids; palatial estate; fast cars; great food; exotic vacations. Now go find those outcomes in scripture. Even King Solomon lost his way with wealth and the Vegas-like accoutrements that accompanied his lifestyle.

The Russians thought their path was accurate then, and Russia and China think their system is the right path now, as do we Americans about our own system. I don't intend to go down a path of which government is right; I'm more interested in how individuals choose a path for the most fulfilling and impactful life. It should look wildly different than the American Dream, and there should be tangible evidence of surrendered service to your fellow man. In other words, hand over the agendas and dreams. There should be no mention of a five-year plan, no seashell collecting on sandy beaches, no never-ending golf excursions upon retirement until you're six feet under. I'm not saying you can't enjoy the culture of fun, but don't make a life of leisure the end goal. While the idea of surrendering dreams might sound horrible and saddening, the Lord who created you might show you dreams to satisfy the deepest recesses of your heart. Isn't that the goal, anyway?

Explore:

1) Are you planning for retirement and a life of leisure or for a life of service and impact?
2) What scares you about abandoning your plans to Jesus Christ? What are the risks?

WEEK 8

MAY THE FORCE BE WITH YOU . . . HOPEFULLY

" 'I ain't a bad guy, just write these little songs
I always pay my union dues, I don't stay in the passing lane'
And he said, 'What about all that whiskey and cocaine' I
said, 'Well, yeah, but that's no reason to throw me in Hell
'Cause I didn't use the cocaine to get high, I just liked the
way it smelled' "

—Ray Wylie Hubbard, *"Conversation with the Devil"*[11]

If left to my own devices, I'll find trouble. You give me five good minutes of allowing my mind to drift wherever it pleases, and I can go all *Dexter* on you in a blink. Hopefully not a full-on serial killer like Michael C. Hall's character in the Showtime series. But watch me on the highway when someone cuts me off in traffic. Sure, sure, I know, we're all "good" people deep down . . . but are we? If you believe scripture is the word of God, it says not so much. In fact, the word used is *depravity*. Total depravity is used to summarize what the Bible teaches about the spiritual condition of fallen man. In modern vernacular, it means we're really effed up at our core and are damn near clueless about it. Which means we have to be vigilant and on guard, because our thoughts will wander and we'll look for trouble due to our brokenness. We'll be damn near clueless about it until we're screaming for a life jacket.

Take, for example, the story of King David in 2 Samuel. In it you'll find the famous story of Israel's king and Bathsheba. The narrative shows the duality of men. We can be great leaders or epic jackasses, and often both, like David. A focus we don't often choose pertains to Uriah the Hittite. Uriah was Bathsheba's husband and one of David's mighty men. He had a life and a story. He gets glossed over because we are drawn to the powerful story of David's failings and attempts to cover up his affair with Bathsheba.

Our culture is built on the idea of winners, or on the underdog who, against all odds, rises to the top. If he or she is humble, shazam! Now we've got tears flowing and all kinds of *feelz*. But Uriah is on the other side of the coin, when God doesn't appear to come through. Uriah got screwed over at the highest level, just by being loyal to the king he trusted and to his wife, who's culpable too. The machinations were beyond his control, and his loyalty cost him his life. I imagine if he would have lived to see David's diabolical maneuverings, he would have been shaking his fist at God and uttering the Hebrew version of WTF!?

This narrative can be a struggle for us as we hope and wait for the Lord to come through in our various pinches, large and small. Uriah is one of those guys where the rainbow and pot of gold don't appear; where prayers appear to be unanswered, or they're answered with an outcome we deem bad. That's the tough stuff and a non-American narrative. We often point to dreams not working out due to lack of effort: "didn't deserve them . . . didn't work hard enough . . . made bad decisions . . . " Did Uriah? Doesn't sound like it. He was faithful to his king, but he got *got* by forces that had nothing to do with his righteousness. And God allowed it.

I'm reminded of an article I read years ago. The publication escapes me, but the article was about an atheist debating a Christian. The atheist stated that his disbelief was due to a magazine cover that showed an African woman carrying her dead child in a barren desert. He was angry with God and said, "All he [God] had to do was make it rain, and the child would've lived. But he didn't. What kind of God is that!?" For sure, our biggest struggle is the same as the atheist's. Children die unexpectedly; people struggle and don't receive any level of relief. Life is unfair one thousand ways all in one day. In other words, we have to trust a God whose love language is Japanese . . . and we only speak Russian.

The tension is equally thick in a spectacular read by Dave Eggers called *What Is the What*. It's based on the story of one of the Lost Boys of Sudan. I had similar feelings as the atheist while reading the tough account of how the children had to escape. While plenty made it out—several ended up employed here in Dallas—I struggled to reconcile the fact that many died from dehydration, and some from lion attacks. And God allowed it.

Years ago, before I recognized my own depravity/effed-upness, I thought, "I would never do anything like David." Then I heard New York City-based Pastor Tim Keller say in a sermon (I'm paraphrasing here), "As soon you say you would never do anything as bad as David . . . you've taken your first step toward doing it." Ouch.

As always, scripture validates the reality. Ephesians 2:1–3 says,

> And you were dead in the trespasses and sins in which you once walked, following the course of this world, following the prince of the power of the air, the spirit that is now at work in the sons of disobedience—among whom we all once lived in the passions of our flesh, carrying out the desires of the body and the mind, and were by nature children of wrath, like the rest of mankind (ESV).

And God allows it.

Explore:

1) Is there a part of your personality or an area in your life where you feel your depravity? If "depravity" is too grandiose a word, in what ways do you fall short?
2) Do you find yourself thinking that other people are much worse than you in terms of integrity and moral character? Does scripture say that certain people are better than others?

WEEK 9

THE BLACK GODFATHER

"I don't let nothing get in my way about anything
I want to do."

—*Clarence Avant*[12]

It seems all of us can start a whackadoo story with the line, "I have an uncle . . . " We pretty much expect a level of kookiness, right? Of course, the proverbial "weird uncle" seems born into every family. So . . . I had an uncle. He often said he was friends with former congressman and Speaker of the House Newt Gingrich. When pressed, his definition of "friendship" meant he lived in Washington, D.C., where Gingrich served, and not at the same time as Gingrich was there, but roughly ten years before. No actual contact. Meh, just details.

Clarence Avant, on the other hand, can claim friendship with Quincy Jones, Jamie Foxx, Michael Jackson, Bill Clinton, Barack Obama, Diddy, Hank Aaron, Bill Withers, Jimmy Jam, Terry Lewis, and a list of others who are indebted to his influence. All of these individuals and more appear in the Netflix documentary *The Black Godfather.* The film is worth its laugh-out-loud weight in gold due to Foxx and his uncanny ability to impersonate anyone, whether speaking or singing.

Clarence is a "rainmaker," a connector of people, who sounds savant-like in his ability to cut through the BS and solve problems. After watching the film, I'm not sure I understand his exact big magic, but clearly he has the ability to silo opposing individuals and help them find a path to the best solution. The dripping adulation of the various celebrities and entertainment CEOs portray a man who is unwavering in his conviction of fair negotiations and equal pay for African Americans. He's influenced the highest echelon of society, including the aforementioned presidents and studio heads David Geffen and Lew Wasserman. In a business known for effing people, as Diddy said, Avant would advise his vast number of friends seeking help to ask for the equivalent fee, royalty, or severance as their white counterparts. Even more fascinating is that Avant is not a Tony Robbins giant of a man. In his younger photos and videos, he doesn't appear physically formidable in any capacity, validated by Al Sharpton in the film.

When I first saw the preview and title, I assumed the story would show a shadowy figure working in the underbelly of entertainment, all seedy and mobbed up. However, the complete opposite occurs; it shows a man bending over backwards to help others. As often as he talks about life being "numbers only," his true purpose shines through.

To a T, everyone in the film says that Avant is fearless, that he has a tenacity to get things done. His ambition also led to near bankruptcy as he overextended himself—a period his daughter describes as when he didn't listen to his friends and his pride got the best of him.

Ah, there's a topic with which to wrestle. The same chutzpah that enabled Avant to kick in the doors of the gatekeepers might also be the thing that leads to downfall. Avant recovered due to his loyal friends helping him out of the financial hole. But the question is when—if ever—should we stop chasing our crazy dreams and pause for reflection? When does the drive to blaze a new trail teeter over into toxic ambition? Rob Siltanen, the creative director at advertising firm TBWA\Chiat\Day, wrote the celebrated commercial that launched Apple's "Think Different" campaign. He penned this classic:

> Here's to the crazy ones. The misfits. The rebels.
> The troublemakers. The round pegs in the square
> holes. The ones who see things differently. They're
> not fond of rules. And they have no respect for
> the status quo. You can quote them, disagree with
> them, glorify or vilify them. About the only thing
> you can't do is ignore them. Because they change
> things. They push the human race forward. And
> while some may see them as the crazy ones, we see
> genius. Because the people who are crazy enough
> to think they can change the world are the ones
> who do.[13]

Gives me chills and feels every time I read it. Amen to all of it . . . as long as the purpose is righteous. A couple of word edits here and there, and you're talking about any number of dictators throughout history. Avant had a singular mission: to advance his race toward equality, he was essentially making disciples, teaching them how to do business with integrity. Kudos to him! There's a poignant scene in the film where a younger executive mentions his call with Avant, in which he told Avant he planned on divorcing his wife. Avant emphatically cursed him out (watch the credits, as everyone speaks to Avant's talent of calling people a muthuhfucka) and convinced him to stay with his wife. Scripture reminds us of how important it is to ensure our compass is pointing north and for our drive to make change to be centered on good missions wired in us from above. Proverbs 3:5–7 says:

> Trust in the LORD with all your heart
> And do not lean on your own understanding.
> In all your ways acknowledge Him,
> And He will make your paths straight.
> Do not be wise in your own eyes;
> Fear the LORD and turn away from evil (NASB).

"Do not be wise in your own eyes." Oh, the tension in that statement! But what about when my gut feels so damn right about a path I'm taking? What about when my heart feels completely invested in a venture, mission, or person? Avant seems to be able to navigate the fog; I hope I can too.

Explore:

1) Do you find yourself trusting your own instincts instead of in the Lord? How do you know when the plan is yours or His?

2) Would you find satisfaction in helping someone who deserves to get ahead if it resulted in you falling behind?

WEEK 10

MY CRUISE SHIP TO FREEDOM

*"But the Hebrew word, the word timshel—'Thou
mayest'—that gives a choice. It might be the most important
word in the world. That says the way is open. That throws it
right back on a man. For if 'Thou mayest'—it is also true
that 'Thou mayest not.'"*

—*John Steinbeck,* East of Eden[14]

Some stories are permanently etched in your mind and provide a
visceral punch to your life card. Here are two of those.

The first was in 2009 on my second trip to Cuba with a damn
impressive organization called Wheels for the World. They provide life-changing mobility, along with the hope of the gospel,
to people impacted by disability worldwide. WFTW is a soup-to-
nuts, well-oiled machine. They collect and refurbish wheelchairs,
working with incarcerated men in American prisons who bring the
chairs back to life. The wheelchairs are then delivered to countries
around the world where social services for the disabled are lacking.

The chairs are custom fitted by medical specialists and then pieced together by mechanics like me to fit the person in need. In this case, the person in need was in Havana, Cuba. That's the warm and fuzzy *feelz* part.

"I have a brother in Minnesota," a local Cuban told me as we looked out over Havana's harbor. I remember giving a Scooby-Doo look of "Hruh?" to the translator. I asked for more detail on how the man's brother made it to Minnesota. Through tearful eyes, he said that his brother and two friends had strung together three inner tubes and floated from Cuba to the Florida Keys. "Wow, that's extraordinary!" I may have held up my hand for a high five. "Are they all doing well there?" I asked. With his head turned down, he mumbled out some quiet words. The translator took a deep breath and said, "The other two friends didn't make it. They were eaten by sharks."

I kind of shuffled and stood there blinking, trying to process what I heard. The Cuban man helped me through my awkwardness. Through the translator, he said, "You don't understand our reality. We're trapped here. We'd rather risk our lives with sharks than be trapped on an island." It was impossible to corral my thoughts. Imagine if your only viable option for a better life was a black inner tube on the open seas? Try to place yourself in their shoes, and you're about to step into an inner tube for a 110-mile journey on open water with sharks lurking below.

The second story comes from trips to Haiti. One image that sticks out was in 2010 after the earthquake that killed 230,000 people in thirty-nine seconds. Driving in Haiti is challenging even without a natural disaster of such magnitude. One day, our two SUVs were making our way through traffic at a clip of about ten to fifteen miles per hour. Alongside us, a shirtless, sweating man came running up next to me on the passenger side, keeping pace with the vehicle. He was balancing a basket on his head that had plastic baggies of water for sale. I rolled down my window, and with the dexterity of an athlete, he reached over his head, grabbed a couple of waters, and handed them to me; then he made change and accelerated to the vehicle in front of ours. I can still see him running in my mind. That was his "career," earning maybe a nickel per bag.

Okay, so what's the point? Not sure. There's a question somewhere in there about placing hope in God when there's no chance of a better life. Would I? Could I? Dunno. At best, is there maybe a smidgen of empathy with those stories? Not really. Those are shoes a thousand miles beyond my feet. Come on—I was born in America, I'm a white male, I'm straight, I have no disability and a decent mind, and my parents were married for fifty-nine years before my dad passed away. How many undeserved lotteries is that compared to folks who were dealt a hand of cards that includes challenges right out of the gate? Will I ever have to deal with racism? Sexism? Homophobia? Lack of opportunity? No way.

Again, why have I been ruminating on Cuba and Haiti the past few days? Perspective? Sure, an easy guess. I often mention a humanitarian aid trip to a friend, and they'll reply, "Gosh, that story makes me *SO* grateful for what I have." Then I say, "And?" In other words, don't just rest in your blessings. What are you doing to impact others? You think we've been awarded our born-in-the-USA lottery ticket to dance the night away? Hell no. I think that's why I get irritated when folks use politics as a reason to not help the non-lottery winners. Peel back all the bullshit rhetoric and it comes down to "Those people don't deserve help." For damn sure this idea doesn't line up with Christ.

In past experience, these Holy Spirit "burdens" I feel about an experience usually push me toward activity—as they should for all of us. We've been wired to serve others, each person turning around to lend a hand up to the next in line. What is the thing that stirs you? Doesn't have to be Cuba; doesn't have to be people. I have a friend who fosters dogs and helps find permanent homes for them. Here's an easy one: how many times do you walk past a homeless person and not make eye contact? I often avoid those situations. What if we used eye contact as a trigger to volunteer at the North Texas Food Bank or Austin Street Center? Take the kids and make the easy two hours a life lesson of seeing all people as worthy of a handshake. Do it regularly—how about four times a year as a starting place. Then next year, instead of a trip to Cabo, go a step further and find a service trip for the family. Email me and I'll help find one for you.

What if my job my whole life was selling thirty to forty bananas each day, or selling thirty to forty bags of water with no other options for provision? I'm reminded of a picture we took with the group of men we were helping. We were in a nicer part of Port-au-Prince at night, and the photo was almost pitch black. Why? There was no electricity. Not "the power was out for the night." There's no electricity 24/7.

I get it. I understand the trepidation when hearing about how serving others is a biblical mandate. People often position the Bible as a great and mighty buzzkill of a rule book. But they miss the entire message by a marathon distance. The entire book is a love letter from God as He tries to woo us back to a relationship with Him. "Uh, whuh . . . ?" That's the Cliff Notes version, but yes . . . over a 1600-year story arc, God is desperately trying to get our attention. This culminates in Him saying, "Hey, if I send my Son to die, which covers all your past, present and future mistakes with ZERO cost to you, will you allow us to get back together and go steady and head to the eternal prom together?" His Son, Jesus, then gives us a couple hunnerd examples of how we can serve others.

> For I was hungry and you gave me food, I was thirsty and you gave me drink, I was a stranger and you welcomed me, I was naked and you clothed me, I was sick and you visited me, I was in prison and you came to me (Matthew 25:35–36 ESV).

Pay attention to the stuff that sparks something in you. Maybe it irritates you because you see wrongs that should be righted. If nothing comes to mind, pray for it. Ask God to place a healthy burden on your heart. Guaranteed He'll plant a seed in your soul that will fill you with a permanent desire to serve someone.

Explore:

1) What cause or issue gets you fired up? Find an organization involved in solving the problem and go volunteer for them.
2) Do you have first-world problems you need to place in proper perspective? A helpful cure is a humanitarian aid trip to a third-world country.

WEEK 11

LOSS OF TEETH = MOXIE

*"Having moxie means having enough cleverness, skill,
creativity, fortitude and cajones to solve (or, at least, to get out
of) a difficult and personally threatening situation."*

—*Urban Dictionary*[15]

Peacocks are an indigenous bird in Dallas, Texas. They populate
many area offices, health clubs, and bars. Haven't seen them?
Actually, we're overrun. At your gym, look for the guy with the
shredded T-shirt hanging off his boulder-esque shoulders by two
small threads, guns a-blazin', massive pecs on display, gallon jug o'
water always nearby. He grunts as he slams his dumbbells on the
mat. Down below, the skinniest little pretzel sticks protrude from
his shorts. Or, in the conference room, he's the one who says, "I
think what you meant to say was [insert condescending redirect]."
Always correcting, never listening. At the bar, he's the one laughing the loudest, yelling at the screen for all to hear. Yep, pretty
much the perfect dudes to never have a beer with. *Peacocking* is one

of my favorite words, as in, "Damn, that dude is peacocking. What a jackass."

Moxie, on the other hand, is pure gold. It doesn't have negative connotations in the same way *pride* and *ambition* do. Both of those words are slippery slopes if not handled with care, like a little girl playing with Mommy's lipstick: cute for a few minutes, but don't go overboard. Urban Dictionary captures moxie well; another dictionary says, "Strength of mind that enables one to endure adversity with courage."[16] Synonyms for *moxie* are *backbone, grit, gumption, guts*, and *fortitude*.

This week I had separate lunches with two friends, both of whom display moxie. Both had stories of getting their teeth kicked in and not quitting on life. For sure, they ended up in the fetal position, but they got back up. There's a consistency to the tribe of folks where humility came to them in the form of an ass-kicking. Whether business failure, adultery, or dreams that died a messy death, the result is fortitude, a deep reservoir of knowing what's real and what's horseshit. Those folks speak about the mystery of God; they recognize human frailty; their language is colored with phrases like "Damned if I know what's going to happen. I hope it works out, but that's above my pay grade." A Dallas peacock is a lost ship in this discussion, at best giving a Hallmark platitude. A peacock thinks he (or she) is the one navigating the chessboard and doesn't recognize their relative "ant-ness" in the grand scheme of things.

I remember having lunch years ago with a gentleman I was speaking with about the possibility of having him step into the role of CEO with a business I was trying to scale. He had a stellar resume as a turnaround specialist with a well-known company in our space. He had also orchestrated an IPO with another company. We met several times, and at our final lunch, I asked him to talk about some of his failures in life. He was seventy-ish years old at the time, so I expected a knowing smile and deep breath before hearing some of the war stories he experienced. Instead, he blinked and asked, "What do you mean?" I tried to reframe the question. "You know, like setbacks, unexpected grenades, personal, business . . . you name it." With an air of affront, he replied, "I haven't had any." And scene. Lunch and relationship concluded. It would've been a near impossibility to work with such a seasoned veteran who believes he's never failed. For clarity, he may not have experienced big loss, which tells me he never took big risks.

As much as I love me some moxie, it's worthwhile to juxtapose it with some of the greatest literature ever transcribed: the Sermon on the Mount, also known as the Beatitudes, from Matthew 5:1–12.

> Now when Jesus saw the crowds, he went up on a mountainside and sat down. His disciples came to him, and he began to teach them.
> He said:

> 'Blessed are the poor in spirit,
>   for theirs is the kingdom of heaven.
> Blessed are those who mourn,
>   for they will be comforted.
> Blessed are the meek,
>   for they will inherit the earth.
> Blessed are those who hunger and thirst for righteousness,
>   for they will be filled.
> Blessed are the merciful,
>   for they will be shown mercy.
> Blessed are the pure in heart,

for they will see God.
Blessed are the peacemakers,
for they will be called children of God.
Blessed are those who are persecuted because
of righteousness,
for theirs is the kingdom of heaven.

'Blessed are you when people insult you, persecute
you and falsely say all kinds of evil against you
because of me. Rejoice and be glad, because great
is your reward in heaven, for in the same way they
persecuted the prophets who were before you.' "

Pretty much everything about the Beatitudes is what's called the
upside-down kingdom of God. A quick Bible study primer: when
scripture repeats the same words in a section, chapter, or book,
it usually means God wants us to pay attention. In this case, it's
blessed. In other words, Jesus is saying, "Wanna be blessed? This is
what it looks like in my world." Our culture lives the opposite of
what Christ is saying in the Sermon on the Mount. I don't want to
be blessed for my weakness, meekness, mourning, and hunger, or
when people insult or persecute me. I don't regularly show mercy,
particularly with people I don't like. Do I hunger and thirst for
righteousness? For moments, but only if it looks favorable to me.
In fact, if I pause and think about what I want on some days, it
looks entirely like a boozy night in Vegas and very little like the
kingdom of God. Can I generate my own moxie? Nope, not without failure. All those synonyms don't come from winning. When
things come too easy, moxie can't exist. Being able to withstand
what Christ is speaking of requires a sort of supernatural peace-
fulness that may move outside the lanes of the definition. It's like

asking a person to create genuine humility. They can't—not without an action from outside of themselves that forces acknowledgement of powerlessness. Aging is an example. Can't control it, and it sure as shit proves our physical weakness.

I often wish we had the option of dismissing the Bible and its challenging content. Many people look past scripture; it has no meaning to their lives. But can we do that? In other words, do we have the authority to say, "These stories don't matter to me; I live life as I see fit"? I like to drill down deep into the history of the document, because there is no piece of literature with as much veracity. Is it reasonable to believe the Bible is essentially a centuries-old version of the telephone game? Maybe a bunch of folks kept passing made-up stories down to the next generation. Not for twenty years, not for 100 years, but for 3,500 years, give or take. That's a helluva viral campaign, passing through centuries, countries, and kings and queens. Sure, it could be that the thirty-nine authors, most of whom didn't know each other (skirting that whole death problem) somehow were able to keep the connectivity and lucidity of the narrative over a 1,600-year period without any divine guidance. Or, there's the option of the Bible being absolutely true, every story, including the Beatitudes preached by Christ, who died and rose again. If that's true, He's your, my, and every peacock's Lord and Savior, and we need the grit, fortitude, and humility to accept that fact.

Explore:

1) In your life, have you been humbled at a level to understand your powerlessness?
2) Do you trust in the idea that God is ultimately guiding all outcomes, whether they're wins or losses?

WEEK 12

I REBEL; THEREFORE [I] EXIST[17]

*"I'm one of the biggest snobs you've ever met, but I hate
elitism and snobs in general. I guess what I hate is being told
that I can't like something. You can't do this? Oh, well, fuck
you, I'm definitely going to do this."* [18]

—*David Chang, Chef and* Ugly Delicious *host*

It seems like over the past eight to ten years or so, chefs have
become the new rock stars. Maybe not full-on ROCK stars, but
certainly a jump up the fame totem pole. For example, I don't
recall people clamoring to get an autograph from a restaurateur
back in the nineties the way we did from a celebrity or pro athlete.
Maybe it was Anthony Bourdain's *Kitchen Confidential: Adventures in
the Culinary Underbelly* (a great read) or the Food Network creation
of chefs battling in the kitchen with laser lighting and dry ice in
the background. Once we got to slo-mo vignettes of chefs walking while contemplating the meaning of olives with a string score?
Boom—we had a new category of idols to worship.

Don't get me wrong, I can fawn with the best of them. I love me some foodie documentaries ALL. DAY. They combine travel, entrepreneurship, artistry, and magic; the latter for sure when you see how fire, spice, and skill create visceral delights. In the Netflix series *Ugly Delicious*, chef David Chang does his version of Bourdain, taking us on food adventures as he ducks into small hovels where a craftsman spends his or her life perfecting a pizza. I love that level of myopic sweat when generating output, whether food, a painting, or a garden. Of course, there's also constant FOMO in the mix. When Chang darts into a hidden restaurant you could miss with a sneeze, I have low-level anxiety of wanting to visit the spot. But hell, I can't even make time to visit all the gems in my Deep Ellum, Dallas 'hood. But that's a tangent I've already covered in my other book. Shameless plug alert.

In other words, I'm asking: how much of ourselves do we lose to become a better person? And how much, if anything, do we hold on to tightly to keep a rebellious spirit? As a Christ follower, scripture tells me this in John 3:30–31:

> He must become greater; I must become less. The one who comes from above is above all; the one who is from the earth belongs to the earth, and speaks as one from the earth. The one who comes from heaven is above all.

Ah, there's the tension between rebellion and submission, and something greater than our vision. I don't like the idea of reducing *me* to a lesser me. I want *my* vision known. What grabbed me in the *Ugly Delicious* episode was the Chang quote above. Like any true mapmaker, he's doing his own thing, and he took his stand when he jumped out on his own with not your average noodle. That part of his rebel nature is what makes any artist, chef, or entrepreneur brilliant: the ability to veer off and risk failure by taking a stab at your vision, critics be damned.

In the John Eldredge book *Beautiful Outlaw*, Eldredge rightly positions Jesus as the rebel He is. It creates more tension for me. Christ didn't hang out with the rock stars of the world; He chose the broken, ragamuffins, and outcasts. He pushed against the establishment (the pretensions of Pharisees and the Roman officials). He invented a miraculous and timeless form of forgiveness known as grace. At the same time, Christ was wholly subservient to the will of His Father. His life was one of complete sacrifice for others on an exponential scale that's difficult to grasp. We forget that His revolutionary teaching came before the Dark Ages. He preached how love conquers all during a time when conquering was only associated with war and death. We've heard 1 Corinthians 13:4–7 so many times at weddings, but we forget the genesis of the message. Keep in mind this was written during a time when women were considered a form of chattel.

> Love is patient, love is kind. It does not envy, it does not boast, it is not proud. It does not dishonor others, it is not self-seeking, it is not easily angered, it keeps no record of wrongs. Love does not delight in evil but rejoices with the truth. It always protects, always trusts, always hopes, always perseveres.

Truly extraordinary words. Could a man make this up without the hand of God? An equally challenging question is: could David Chang keep his rebellious spirit while being surrendered to the greater will of Jesus? Can you? It's a battle I fight daily. Lord, help me know deep in my heart that your rebellion is the one that counts.

Explore:

1) Is it difficult for you to consider sacrificing your goals and agenda in sacrifice to others?
2) Did you grow up with a vision of Jesus as a righteous rebel, or did you have a misinformed definition that sounded like buzzkill?

WEEK 13

THE INTOXICATION OF BENJAMINS

"There's no way that Michael Jackson or whoever Jackson should have a million thousand droople billion dollars, and then there's people starving. There's no way! There's no way that these people should own planes and there are people who don't have houses. Apartments. Shacks. Drawers. Pants! I know you're rich. I know you got forty billion dollars, but can you just keep it to one house? You only need one house. And if you only got two kids, can you just keep it to two rooms? I mean why have fifty-two rooms and you know there's somebody with no rooms? It just don't make sense to me. It don't." [19]

—*Tupac Shakur*

One of my favorite pastors and authors is Tim Keller. He's on the Mount Rushmore of theology for me, along with Brennan

Manning, Anne Lamott, C. S. Lewis, and John Eldredge. Keller has had some funny moments in his sermons over the years where he mentions movies he watches any time they're on: *Back to the Future* is one. To him, the theology of Marty Mcfly resonates. Who am I to argue with TK? I'm the same way with Martin Scorsese's *Goodfellas*, the Coen Brothers' *No Country for Old Men*, and Francis Ford Coppola's *Apocalypse Now*. I'll watch them over and over; they're utterly intoxicating due to the characters, dialogue, artistry, music scores, and the emotions that bubble up during the ride.

There are also movies and programs I try to avoid—or, at least, I have to ensure my compass is pointing north while watching. *Californication* is one; *Entourage* is another. Both have too much sex and cool circumstances that could send my mind on a bender. Music has that effect too; songs by Mazzy Star, Jeff Buckley, and Radiohead can transport me to a melancholy hotel where I can't stay. Everyone has their unique kryptonite, and those are some of mine. I had a buddy once who couldn't listen to Pink Floyd or The Doors because their music made him think about weed too much . . . and he liked him some weed at breakfast, lunch, and dinner.

The Showtime program *Billions* is another one of those shows for me. Oh Lordy, like catnip for dudes! Let's see . . . it includes heavy doses of power, manipulation, wealth, domination of an opponent, and the various accouterments that come with winning at all costs. I can watch it, but after each episode I have to remind myself of what's important as a Christ follower. The characters speak clever dialogue we wish we could produce in the heat of the moment, but in reality only exist because of a brilliant script writer. It's fun to keep up with the various pop culture and music references peppered throughout, sorta like Tarantino in many of his films. It also seems that many of the male characters are required to deliver their lines in a sinister, whispery baritone. Criminy, it's like TV crack. Plus, Damian Lewis has reached the level where he can read a Starbucks menu for two hours and make it compelling.

For me, the barometer is a question of which option revs me up—the darkness of *Billions* or the idea of volunteering at a homeless shelter? *That's* where we tell on ourselves. I have to choose to serve, to volunteer, to give to others. My natural inclination is to let Vegas rule and let all that fun darkness wash over me. Thankfully, I now have a healthy blood flowing inside known as the Holy Spirit. It cleanses those desires and helps me see them for what they are: not the best outcome if I let them run rampant.

Before I run down a biblical tangent, I want to preface my points. For one, God is a worker; God wants us to work hard, using all the gifts He's given us. He wants our work to be a collaboration with Him, and He started this in the very beginning when He gave Adam his first action items: naming the animals in Genesis 2:19–20.

> Now the LORD God had formed out of the ground all the wild animals and all the birds in the sky. He brought them to the man to see what he would name them; and whatever the man called each living creature, that was its name. So the man gave names to all the livestock, the birds in the sky and all the wild animals.

The Lord also gives us clear boundaries regarding how wealth can take our eyes off the prize. The parable of the seeds is in all three Synoptic Gospels; I prefer Luke's version due to the word *pleasures*. Luke 8:14 says:

> The seed that fell among thorns stands for those
> who hear, but as they go on their way they are
> choked by life's worries, riches and pleasures, and
> they do not mature.

In the parable, Christ is saying the seeds of what's important in life are planted in us (the "seed" being the Word of God). Boom. Right there I've already lost 40% of the people reading this. "Come on. Bible crap!? Buzzkill. Whomp whomp." Ah, but the richness of scripture is how damn timeless it is. The parable of the seeds has three examples of how the important things in life get snatched away or don't take root when tested by hard times; the third, which relates to *Billions*, is the "worries, riches and pleasures" we encounter. Scripture talks about money being *A* root of evil, not *THE* root, as often misquoted (1 Timothy 6:10 NASB). That's why I say work is good and money is good as an endeavor and commodity. But money, sex, and booze seem to be the things that grab hold of us like a constrictor. Actually, it's the opposite: we grab them and squeeze as much life out of them as we can, not realizing our lives are being consumed.

Which is what makes *Billions* so damn seductive. I'm lying if I say I don't care about winning; that I don't care about having more money, sex, and influence than another guy; that I don't want to be known as a powerful man. If I don't have scripture as a compass, what do I use as my navigator? I have friends who say culture steers them. Yikes—try finding the right direction in our current climate. What about inner fortitude? All well and fine until you realize how often your gut feelings are wrong (read Malcolm Gladwell's *Blink* for examples).

The slide towards ineffectiveness is subtle. In other words, if I'm not consciously making choices that sacrifice my mighty agenda, I'll slide into a cozy American Dream lifestyle, the nice vacations, the bigger home. Again, not saying leave your career behind, not saying vacations are bad. But what if your life looked like some of the doctors I met on Mercy Ships who worked three months out of the year while serving on Mercy Ships for nine? They didn't leave their careers; they simply shifted focus to things of eternal value and kept influences like *Billions* in their proper place as entertainment only and not a life goal.

Explore:

1) What in this world is the most seductive for you? Fame? Wealth? Sex? Have you found any of them to be the answer to all of life's worries?

2) Is service or volunteering a mainstay of your life? Do you lead and encourage your family to include service as an obligation of being a good citizen?

WEEK 14

IT'S MY TIMELINE, DAMMIT!

"Impatience is racing at misery full speed." [20]

—*Richelle E. Goodrich,* Slaying Dragons

Americans are by far some of the most patient people on earth . . . said no one ever.

I'm in a men's Bible study group. Yesterday, we discussed how to be impeccable with our words. Essentially, we asked questions like "When does busting each other's chops go over the line and become more of a personal jab?" There were a handful of anecdotal stories where we didn't live up to our good intentions. I and another guy both mentioned how we stupidly flip people off when someone cuts us off in traffic. We tried to justify it as "righteous indignation," but we couldn't find a single damn verse in scripture to cherry-pick to justify our conclusion. Hate when scripture doesn't conform to my driving needs.

This morning I continued thinking about that discussion while reading 2 Kings 21—an Old Testament book, and not exactly a page-turner. First and 2 Kings are basically a 340-year timeline of the leaders of the Northern and Southern kingdoms of Israel. No need to get super biblical, since it quickly goes above my pay grade as a non-scholar. The primary theme is how God is faithful even during wretched leadership by the majority of the kings after David and Solomon.

What grabbed me about 2 Kings 21 was the mention of Manasseh becoming king at the age of twelve and ruling for fifty-five years. My eyes bug out at the idea of a little punko 6th-grader ruling a nation, even if he was like Lady Mormont in *Game of Thrones*, which he wasn't. What stood out is the timeline of fifty-five years. We don't have patience for waiting. A crap king ruling for fifty-five years would be dreadful, but bad leadership or corrupt government is not my point.

> "How long must I wait . . . for my cup of coffee?"
> (2 Coffee 7:12)

I would love to see if peeps are frantically searching their Bible for the Book of Coffee, but I digress. Waiting is what captures my imagination. 340 years of not-so-good circumstances, fifty-five years of bad leadership, or the 400 years of biblical silence between Malachi and Matthew. I want things to happen when I say so. That would be yesterday on most items. Whether it's the barista at Starbucks, the car in front of me, or the Amazon delivery not happening till the end of the day . . . you're *all* screwing with my clock! Impatience seems to be the human condition, and God often uses time as His tactic to rid us of that habit. Is it only an American issue? Not sure. I can speak loosely to certain cultures—India, for example—where, on my visits, the pace felt as frenetic as 5 p.m. in Manhattan.

But what does it take for us to realize our limitations of time? The deeper question seems to be one of control. Because of our affluence and technological advancement, do we create a false sense of control? A few successes under our belt, no bad health scares, and shazam, I am the master of my destiny. Here's a passage that fascinates me on multiple levels: Luke 13:10–13.

> On a Sabbath Jesus was teaching in one of the synagogues, and a woman was there who had been crippled by a spirit for eighteen years. She was bent over and could not straighten up at all. When Jesus saw her, he called her forward and said to her, "Woman, you are set free from your infirmity." Then he put his hands on her, and immediately she straightened up and praised God.

The part about "eighteen years" caught my attention last year, and I began noticing other parts of scripture where waiting is required. You'll find many verses pertaining to long periods of waiting and suffering while the clock ticks. In those Luke verses, it's not as if the woman should've tried yoga to straighten her posture. She had what was likely perceived as a health issue. Turns out it was actually an evil spirit, which Christ says in verse 16 came from Satan. While the miracle of her healing happened *immediately*, she had eighteen years of struggle before that healing, and God allowed it. Plenty of people don't get the miracle healing; they can only live out a timeline not of their making.

Or how about Job, one of the most daunting books in scripture? We don't receive as much detail on the timeline, but we definitely learn there's much going on behind the spiritual curtain. The gist of the book is a poker game between Satan and the Lord. One of the lessons in Job is how blatantly wrong Job's three friends are in assessing his life circumstances. In so many words, they're saying, "Look, bro, you must've screwed this up due to bad choices or some other thing you're hiding. Fess up!" How many times have I done the same with my friends? For clarity, I'm not referring to the obvious, like "Knocking over a string of liquor stores will not solve your money woes." I'm talking about how we use our wisdom to fix circumstances that might be ordained from the Lord. Discerning when God wants us to sit and stew in some struggle is a bitch of the highest order. Our culture is not prone to sit idly for a life lesson from the Lord. We want sales to happen now to make our nut, or a relationship to be fixed within a month. We don't have the wisdom and patience to wait on the Lord's timing.

How much do we miss when we shoot from the hip and try to fix a thing based on the chessboard in front of us? We didn't maneuver the players to their positions, we didn't invent the game, and we sure as hell don't control the clock. In other words, all the circumstances we think our Mensa prowess engineered are actually part of God's plan, including the bad seasons that never seem to end.

Can I learn to be patient during the struggles while the clock ticks away? Based on how many drivers I flipped off this year, that would be a no.

Explore:

1) Can you recall a time in your life when you did and didn't practice patience? In each case, how did things turn out? Did God reveal anything to you in either case?
2) Does Romans 8:28 help you hold the tension of trusting the brilliance of God as He moves the chess pieces in your life?

WEEK 15

TRUTHINESS AIN'T WHAT IT USED TO BE (PART 1 OF 3)

" 'The truth.' Dumbledore sighed. 'It is a beautiful and terrible thing, and should therefore be treated with great caution.' " [21]

—J. K. *Rowling,* Harry Potter and the Sorcerer's Stone

When I speak, you can guaran-damn-tee it's truth! . . . or, at least, *my* version of truth . . . which kinda makes it an opinion . . . but anyway, it's damn true!

That's the climate we live in now. If I take a position on an issue, I want it sorta fluid and malleable, and if it offends, then clearly it's wrong. Therefore, the best thing for all of us is to create a truth that works for each individual and let everyone do their own thing. Cool, let's close in prayer, discussion done.

But does that thesis hold up? In my first book, *I'm Not Hitler,* I have a chapter titled "No Absolute Truthiness," stealing from Stephen Colbert's brilliant character on his show *The Colbert Report.*

He was genius as a political commentator who spoke in a sort of pseudo-truth. Ah, if only we could laugh him away as silly ol' TV. Now we have non-fictitious political operatives who work with what's known as alternative facts and "truth isn't truth." Nope, not gonna jab at one political party over another; both sides of the aisle are no different than all of us wanting to build our own narrative truth.

Let me set some foundation. In two national surveys conducted by Barna Group, one among adults and one among teenagers, people were asked if they believe there are moral absolutes that are unchanging, or that moral truth is relative to the circumstances. By a 3-to-1 margin (64% vs. 22%), adults said truth is always relative to the person and their situation.[22] The perspective was even more lopsided among teenagers, 83% of whom said moral truth depends on the circumstances and only 6% of whom said moral truth is absolute.[23]

This is a new phenomenon. In the past, the ancient Greek origins of the words "true" and "truth" had consistent definitions throughout great spans of history. Topics such as logic, geometry, mathematics, deduction, induction, and natural philosophy were considered unbending truth. In Hinduism, truth is defined as "unchangeable," "that which has no distortion," "that which is beyond distinctions of time, space, and person," and "that which pervades the universe in all its constancy."[24]

Why does truth matter? Because without a solid framework, we dismiss God's authority as the creator and originator of truth or we place Him in a subservient position where He bows to our version of truth that works for us.

(Yawn). Still don't care? Try this on. Without a pure standard that's never diluted, I could say something like this: "In my truth, there are different races and ethnicities who are inferior." Whuh?

That's not right! I can't say that! This is where the Greek logic comes into play. If I follow the Barna study that says moral truth is relative, then the game has no rules; we just make 'em up as we go. In other words, if relative truth existed, then it'd be totally cool to be a racist and no one would object. Or if I said "lock up all Christians," there would be no outcry because all truths are equal, there is no right and wrong, and we all eat cupcakes happily ever after. Let's stick with the racism illustration since it's an issue that's right in front of us daily. The fact that most people *do* recognize a racist statement as inherently wrong points us toward a greater truth that sets the standard. You might think that everyone knows racism is evil. I would hope so, but history paints a portrait where desires for master races (such as those held by the Nazis or the Khmer Rouge) lead to genocide solely based on misguided opinions masked as truth. I witnessed the aftermath firsthand on a 2004 trip to Kigali, Rwanda, ten years after the 1994 genocide. There I saw a graveyard the size of eight football fields, with wooden caskets stacked six deep in a cavernous chamber under a metal floor. In that cemetery alone, there were 250,000 bodies out of the estimated 750,000 people who were murdered in the span of ninety days. Yes . . . ninety days.

We're often cavalier about having a firm compass for our hearts and minds. But there's kindling in every part of the world waiting to spark. Here's the reality. In Kigali, before the genocide turned people against each other, they were neighbors living in homes next door to each other, people from the same country with the same skin tone. Smouldering heat can turn deadly on a mass scale, and ninety days later, hundreds of thousands of people were dead, with generations impacted for decades. I wrongly assumed that the Tutsi and Hutu tribes had been warring for centuries, like people groups in the Middle East. Nope. The toxicity began with the colonialism of white Belgians and Germans in the early to mid-1900s. The spark turned into a blazing fire in 1994.

> Rwanda's colonial period, during which the rul-
> ing Belgians favored the minority Tutsis over the
> Hutus, exacerbated the tendency of the few to
> oppress the many, creating a legacy of tension that
> exploded into violence even before Rwanda gained
> its independence.[25]

Maybe Rwanda seems too far away, too third-world. Fair enough; how about this hot-button issue? A big chunk of our country thinks it's 100% morally accurate for a woman to have control of her body and have the authority to abort a fetus. Another equally large group of Americans believes with 100% fervor that the fetus is a child with legitimacy and must be protected. Can both sides be right?

Yesterday was the fifth anniversary of the death of Eric Garner. When truth is muddy, justice gets messy. As a white male, it'd be golly-darn convenient for me to be dismissive of his death because I've never had to deal with a smidgen of racial profiling. If I carry that dismissiveness in conversation while grabbing beers with black friends, now I've added to the kindling. Why? Because their truth is theirs and mine is mine.

Whuh!? In one sentence, I've taken identical humans with two hands, two eyes, the same brain and emotions—*one race*—with only melanin count as the difference and tried to separate us into subcategories of "us" and "them." I could spin off twenty different directions separating ethnicities and form jackass definitions of "truths" that work for each ethnicity, which would introduce inequalities. I could throw in some "nationality" too for an extra layer of "truths." And that would only prove one thing . . . I'm a jackass.

How about the fact that the Democratic party is by far the best political choice when weighing all the facts on all important issues? Or the fact that the Republican party is head and shoulders the only political choice when drilling down into the truth of America? Can both sides be right on all issues?

Or with that pesky thing called religion. Everyone knows that Islam, Hinduism, Christianity, and Buddhism are all the same. No need to argue . . . plus, being an atheist or spiritual and non-religious works too. Can they all be right?

Explore:

1) Do you struggle with the concept of God as the source of absolute truth?

2) If we all have our own truth, how do we determine if any person's truth is false?

WEEK 16

WHO'S YOUR TRUE NORTH?
(PART 2 OF 3)

*"Facts do not cease to exist because
they are ignored."* [26]

—*Aldous Huxley*

You've probably heard the phrase "true north." The Wikipedia definition says, "True north (also called geodetic north) is the direction along Earth's surface towards the geographic North Pole or True North Pole."[27]

The scientific version is blah. But when we use the phrase "true north" in conversation, we're saying that the subject we're referring to is "solid" or "accurate." For example, if I mention a fireman and say, "Those folks have their compasses pointed true north," I'm saying that they stand for safety and integrity and that they know exactly what their mission is.

Let's think of true north in that context for today in relation to truth. Seems pretty straightforward that we would respect people who stand for something, the ones who keep their word, who have weathered the storms of life and are reliable. I would posit that those folks also have a selflessness to them, an outwardness to their disposition. Therefore, the opposite of true north might be "flaky." There's no consistency, no stability in the person's direction, and you can't get a read on 'em. Might say, "Something about them seems shady—can't pin them down."

Do you want to surround yourself with friends who are of "true north" character? Or do you prefer the flaky ones you can't trust and probably won't call when you're in a pickle at 2 a.m.? Side note and true story—twenty years ago, a friend called me at 2 a.m. and asked me to pick up his girlfriend from jail . . . because he was too tired. I was flabbergasted, but my shock was thimble-esque compared to that of his girlfriend when *I* showed up, *not him*, to gather her from Dallas County's Lew Sterrett. The look of utter disappointment on her face is permanently etched in my mind. My buddy wasn't a dirtbag. He made a poor choice in the moment, same as I have fifty or more times in other scenarios.

Is there someone current or historical you look to as an example of solid truth? Abraham Lincoln comes to mind. Teddy Roosevelt. Nelson Mandela. Or you could say your true north is the letter of the law. Maybe, if pressed further, you might say your highest truth is the Constitution of the United States. Now we're getting somewhere interesting. The Constitution was ratified in 1788, more than a decade after the Declaration of Independence was written. In the latter document, we find these inspired words:

> "We hold these truths to be self-evident, that all men are created equal, that they are endowed by **their Creator** with certain unalienable rights, that among these are Life, Liberty and the Pursuit of happiness." These stirring words were designed

to convince Americans to put their lives on the line for the cause. Separation from the mother country threatened their sense of security, economic stability, and identity. The preamble sought to inspire and unite them through the vision of a better life.[28]

Boom! That has some horsepower! I purposely bolded "their Creator." The founding fathers started with God as their foundation, as their true north. No need to volley back and forth who among the founding fathers was Christian and who was only deist. The main point is you'll find no reputable writing of any of them being devout atheists. Even Ben Franklin says this:

"Here is my Creed," Franklin wrote to [Ezra] Stiles [the Calvinist president of Yale College]. "I believe in one God, Creator of the Universe. That He governs it by His Providence. That he ought to be worshiped. That the most acceptable Service we render to him, is doing Good to his other Children. That the Soul of Man is immortal, and will be treated with Justice in another Life respecting its Conduct in this. . . . As for Jesus of Nazareth . . . I think the system of Morals and Religion as he left them to us, the best the World ever saw . . . but I have . . . some Doubts to his Divinity; though' it is a Question I do not dogmatism upon, having never studied it, and think it is needless to busy myself with it now, where I expect soon an Opportunity of knowing the Truth with less Trouble."[29]

Any document or book we point to as the best truth to use as our compass has ultimately been authored by mankind. Yes, the Quran, Torah, and Bible were all authored by people. Those holy books claim to be "God-breathed," meaning they were inspired by God working through the men and women picking up the pen and parchment. By the way, I have to chuckle when my non-believing friends say, "I don't believe any holy book that was made up by man." They then proceed to give me their version of spirituality they use for truth . . . which was authored by him or her, who also happens to be a person.

This is where we segue back to the previous chapter regarding your truth is yours, mine is mine, and tragic results related to Rwanda, Eric Garner, and abortion. What's the connection? Every issue—failed marriage, famine, lack of access to clean water, mental illness, alcoholism, race relations—all have proponents claiming true north. Abortion is no different; both sides claim to hold the accurate truth. Guaranteed neither side will wake up one day and say, "You know, come to think of it, I'm okay with what they believe." They cannot both be true because their positions contradict each other, and the law of non-contradiction debunks two opposites both being true.

I had a conversation recently where I said that every war in the Middle East and every humanitarian aid challenge would be solved if Jesus Christ returned tomorrow. Yep, there were easily five seconds of blank stares from my friends. They blinked in awe at my newfound Martian status. Stay with me here. As a Christ follower, I'm called and commanded to believe what the Holy Bible says. It unambiguously states that Christ lived, died, rose again, ascended to heaven, and will return. As the literal definition of pure truth, He will fix our busted, effed-up world and continue His role as Creator, Governor, Owner, Big Cheese, El Hefe, and

Grand Poobah of the entire universe. For clarity, I didn't accept this concept blindly. I dug deep and fought hard to disprove the whole idea of Christ, but eventually had to tap out because the Bible was and is astoundingly powerful. For an intense wrestling starter kit, read *Mere Christianity* by C. S. Lewis and *The Case for Christ* by Lee Strobel, former atheist and former legal editor of *The Chicago Tribune*, as well as my first book, *I'm Not Hitler.*

A good friend and mentor said that offering Christ as the end-all-be-all solution to suffering is considered reductionist. Correct. While the natural world is infinitely complex, the issues I'm discussing can be broken down into ever smaller pieces that are ultimately human, as in "relational." Christ is first and foremost about healing relationships, first with God, then between people.

If I don't perceive Christ as the alpha-and omega-solution of all global problems we face—sickness, dysfunction, morality, racism, wars (whether civil or global)—then I have to look elsewhere for the solution. And what is that other solution? Seriously, what's the answer? "Well, if we would all get our shit together and try harder to be nice people, then things will right themselves" or "If we would continue leveraging science and technology, then the answers will eventually happen and we'll finally get life right." In the former scenario, we're hoping that if world leaders can assemble and agree on all the major issues, then we'll solve everything. But (and that's a big ol' but, for sure) what if those world leaders are each working from their own version of truth that works for them as individuals? This isn't a "what if," it's a fact; they are all working from their own truth. Russia has a nationalistic truth; China does too, as does France, and as do we in the USA. And this is only politics. If we narrow in on health issues, can the collective scientific community get together and nail down the solution for global warming, cancer, clean water for all . . . hell, even the common cold? Let me be clear: I'm not saying there are never any geopolitical, medical, or scientific breakthroughs that fix specific problems. But with medicine in particular, it seems like throwing a pill at the latest syndrome may result in side effects that include nausea, insomnia, vomiting, loss of appetite, dizziness, and loss of sex drive . . . which all require another pill.

This is the problem with pluralism. We may claim that ten truths or 100 truths can all work, but the life issues above make a strong case that multiple truths don't work. Yes, we are functioning, but we are not performing perfectly, and I and others would argue that not only are we not competent, we're failing.

Maybe you're scratching your head and thinking, "Damn, stop being such an alarmist. I've got it pretty good and life's not that bad. Plus, what exactly is the point?" Progress has been made on some fronts, but take a gander at some of the world global statistics at Lifewater. The folks living out those statistics would not say life is peachy. We, as the winners, always have skewed vision because we're not struggling to find food and clean water every day.

Here's a simple example of true north, particularly for a meat-head jock like me. In any sport, there are rules to govern the game. Everyone playing and watching understands how the score is kept and the outcome derived. When a dispute occurs, all participants can look to the guidelines for clarity. If needed, the final authority comes from a governing body who renders a decision.

Can my sports analogy apply to all global issues? Since no person or government can declare that they are the final authority, what or who is the next option? Ultimately, the solution to all woes will be God weaving His magic. It will be Him providing a standard set of guidelines upon which all of us agree. Has the supernatural fix already arrived in the form of Hinduism, Islam, Judaism, or Christianity? Or has God decided that a "spiritual" label and no religious affiliation is the best path? Can all religions be right and true? Or is there a single path God wants us to choose, and He's made it as easy as accepting a free lunch from a friend?

Explore:

1) If you struggle with the idea of a singular truth, can you define at what point one thousand different truths cross over to being wrong?

2) Would it be easier to have a thousand different religions, all with contradictory doctrines? Or is a more effective option to have one path?

WEEK 17

WHY I WORSHIP SATAN
(PART 3 OF 3)

"The greatest trick the devil ever pulled was convincing the world he didn't exist." [30]

—Roger *"Verbal" Kint,* The Usual Suspects

Pluralism regarding truth sounds pleasant. It gives us a feeling of being open-minded and non-judgemental. "You live your life, I live mine, we each stay in our lanes, and we'll all be fine." That works when we're talking about a favorite sports team or whether mustard or ketchup is the best condiment on hot dogs. But with something as crucial as truth, we gotta tighten up any cracks to prevent leaks.

I firmly believe in a biblical worldview that says the world is irrevocably broken. We, as the top of the food chain and stewards of the world, are not capable of fixing all the sickness, addictions, hunger, warring nations, climate issues, and on and on. Our hubris may say otherwise, but the evidence is to the contrary. The Bible is the most lucid explanation of why there's sickness; why people have short life spans; why we're angry, jealous, lustful, and selfish; and why we're loving, gracious, creative, logical, and responsive to inspiration. It also explains why we're incapable of acting as doctors air-dropping a perfect world order from a rescue helicopter.

As I asked in part 2 of 3 of this series, how can religion or a holy book be the solution to all the world's problems? I said that governments cannot agree because they all have their own nationalistic truths which, when parsed, ultimately show how individuals want to live their own truth that works for them. But how do we know when a person's truth steps out of bounds? There must be a final authority for all people to look to as judge and jury on all things good and bad.

How do we know the Bible is the only truth? What about Islam, Hinduism, Judaism, and Buddhism? What proof is there that Christianity is the only truth from God? Plus, isn't that exclusionary? I'm not saying other religious books don't have *any* truth; I'm saying only one can have absolute truth. When I was a new Christ follower, I had questions about one path up the mountain to God versus many paths. Aren't they all leading to the same place? The biggest challenge with that idea is the fact that all the major religions have contradictory doctrines. They do have similar moral overtures, but at their baselines, they're radically different. Let's just stick with the big five for a moment. One says Jesus Christ died and rose again and is the only Son of God—that's Christianity. Judaism and Islam don't believe in the resurrection. Hinduism believes Christ is one of thousands of gods, and that concept contradicts the idea of monotheism within Islam, Judaism, and Christianity. Buddha never claimed to be a deity. That's a starting place on the multiple differences, but the hurdle is the fact that contradictory things cannot all be right. Either all are wrong or one is right, but not all of them are right at the same time. However, the ginormous discrepancies between Christianity and other religions is that the former offers a free gift, no strings attached. You believe in Christ, you get your ticket punched to heaven. His death for us was free; it cost us nothing. For realz. That's it. He did all the work, and the only requirement from us is a big ol' thank you.

This morning, I was driving to work and thinking about what elements I wanted to include in the final part of the truth series. On the radio an NPR story, "This Supreme Court Case Made School District Lines A Tool For Segregation," hit home, and it directly relates to why absolute truth is important. The story is about a significant Supreme Court case from 1974, *Milliken v. Bradley*, roughly twenty years after the landmark case *Brown v. Board of Education*. It dealt with the planned desegregation of public school students among fifty-three school districts in metropolitan Detroit. The NPR story brilliantly captures the issue in a seven-minute listen. In a law review article, I found the dissenting opinion on the 5-4 decision from Justice Thurgood Marshall.

> School district lines, however innocently drawn, will surely be perceived as fences to separate the races when, under a Detroit-only decree, white parents withdraw their children from the Detroit city schools and move to the suburbs in order to continue them in all-white schools.[31]

The long and short of the story is that this result reaffirmed the national pattern of city schools attended mostly by blacks with surrounding suburban schools mostly attended by whites and the disproportionate allocation of funds that has carried over to the present day. This case is one of thousands brought before the Supreme Court, and *Milliken v. Bradley* resulted in a 5-4 decision, not a unanimous 9-0 decision. In other words, the men and women we've decided are the smartest of the smart are rarely able to agree on the most important issues facing our country. Please hear me—our democracy is wonderful and our Supreme Court is the greatest in the world at using civil discourse to decide an issue. But even they need a supreme authority larger than a human brain's capacity.

So why do I worship Satan, and what does that have to do with truth, education, or racism? A dear friend sent me a sermon by Jonathan Pokluda at Harris Creek Church in Waco, Texas. His theology is spot-on, and in this sermon he was preaching from the New Testament book of James in relation to wisdom. During the sermon, he said, "Self-serving wisdom is satanic."[32] I rolled my eyes and thought, *Come on, that's a bit extreme.* He then mentioned how he drew his conclusion based on *The Book of Satan.* I had no idea there was such a book. The author is Anton LaVey. He wrote *The Satanic Bible* in 1969, and while there has been scholarly evaluation of his work, he's not a household name. I doubt you'll find millions of followers in cities around the globe all reveling in their wonderful life changes from reading his book. There isn't a Satanic church on every corner saying, "We got spirit, yes we do, we got spirit, how about you?" In other words, there appears to be significant evidence that the history of Christianity has bigger magic than LaVey's obscure narrative. I'm confident in saying his version of truth will not resonate over centuries, continents, and dynasties the way Christ has. Mind you, the life he describes is one we must juxtapose with scripture.

The Book of Satan suggests a hedonistic outlook, saying, "I break away from all conventions that do not lead to my earthly happiness." Indulgence is endorsed, and readers are encouraged to make the most of their lives. It criticizes both law and religious principles, instead suggesting doing only what makes one happy and successful.[33]

That caught me off-guard. I expected the narrative to say, "Drink blood at midnight. . . People can turn into dragons. . . Place hand grenades in snow cones!" Nope, it basically says to go live a great life that is entirely self-focused and pursue happiness at all costs. Uh, that's what I do often, like pretty much every day. I constantly have to fight my inclination to follow a self-focused path. Therefore, if I do dismiss religious books, cut corners where I can, and use culture as my zeitgeist, my truth could look like the life suggested in *The Book of Satan*.

The Book of Satan validates my original point about pluralism. Since we don't view LaVey's version of truth as legitimate, there must be something inside us pointed toward true north. If this were not the case, we would be morally okay with Satanism, racism, and the pillaging of poodles (I assume evil deeds toward poodles must be somewhere in the Satan book.)

Let me be very clear; I do believe in the Satan who's mentioned in the Bible. I don't believe he's a make-believe boogeyman to scare the kiddos. I believe scripture when it says he is alive behind the invisible curtain and working as our most diligent enemy with an extensive army. Read 1 Peter 5:8, one of many verses about the fallen angel.

> Be alert and of sober mind. Your enemy the devil prowls around like a roaring lion looking for someone to devour.

I'm diligent about seeking truth in relation to all substantive issues, including the feasibility of Anton LaVey's Satan or the Bible's Satan. I try to ask rigorous questions, study what scholars and atheist authors say, and use logic when evaluating stories of heart change. I encourage you to do the same. In fact, go wrestle with these verses from Colossians 1:15–20.

> The Son is the image of the invisible God, the firstborn over all creation. For in him all things were created: things in heaven and on earth, visible and invisible, whether thrones or powers or rulers or authorities; all things have been created through him and for him. He is before all things, and in him all things hold together. And he is the head of the body, the church; he is the beginning and the firstborn from among the dead, so that in everything he might have the supremacy. For God was pleased to have all his fullness dwell in him, and through him to reconcile to himself all things, whether things on earth or things in heaven, by making peace through his blood, shed on the cross.

Fer freak's sake, those verses are some heavy text. I will bridle my desire to drop some holy f-bombs at how significant they are. That's why I say Christ's return is the only solution to all the world's problems. Christ is either THE MAN, or all those churches around the world with hundreds of millions of followers worshiping Him are utterly delusional and insane . . . me included. Dismissing that 2,000-year-old text is disingenuous. You can wrestle with belief and ask questions, but outright dismissal means you've arm-wrestled the most brilliant philosophers, kings, and intellectuals throughout the centuries who've taken a knee in reverential worship. Let's make you famous. See if your version of truth holds up to theirs, which has been personified as Jesus Christ. If you can disprove Christ, you'll be the most famous person in the history of the world, bar none, game over. Your truth will be bigger than The Beatles, more popular than Facebook and Instagram, and more important than the smartphone or Einstein's Theory of General Relativity. You alone will be the new true north.

Explore:

1) Does your life look more like what's described in *The Book of Satan*, focused on happiness and success? Or are you sacrificial and others-focused, as scripture recommends and often commands?

2) Are there obstacles stopping you from believing in Christ? Are the answers to your questions available from respected theologians and scholars?

WEEK 18

WHAT KIND OF
FRIEND ARE YOU?

*"There is nothing like puking with somebody to make you
into old friends."* [34]

—*Sylvia Plath,* The Bell Jar

In the Showtime documentary *Kobe Bryant's Muse*, we see the former NBA superstar under sparse lighting, looking directly into the camera as he discusses his life. He covers his trajectory from the son of an NBA player to a lonely child growing up in Italy to an elite sports assassin with the nickname "Black Mamba." Cool! We respect talent; we're often in awe of it. Whether it's a musician, an athlete, an actor, or a businessperson, when someone moves past mere competency to a level we're incapable of reaching, we step back and applaud. As we should. Mastery of talent always requires work: there must be tenacity, mental and physical sweat, anguish, and failure. If you've attempted to climb the mountain in any field or endeavor, you know all those ingredients are required—no shortcuts. Kudos to Kobe for being an elite among elites.

In the film, he touches on the topic of friendship, which reminded me of a *GQ* article from 2015, "Kobe Bryant Will Always Be an All-Star of Talking." The journalist asked him about friends.

> I have "like minds." You know, I've been fortunate to play in Los Angeles, where there are a lot of people like me. Actors. Musicians. Businessmen. Obsessives. People who feel like God put them on earth to do whatever it is that they do. Now, do we have time to build great relationships? Do we have time to build great friendships? No. Do we have time to socialize and to hangout aimlessly? No. Do we want to do that? No. *We want to work.* I enjoy working.
>
> **So is this a choice? Are you actively *choosing* not to have friends?**
>
> Well, yes and no. I have friends. But being a "great friend" is something I will never be. I can be a *good* friend. But not a *great* friend. A great friend will call you every day and remember your birthday. I'll get so wrapped up in my shit, I'll never remember that stuff. And the people who are my friends understand this, and they're usually the same way. You gravitate toward people who are like you. . . . But in terms of having one of those great, bonding friendships—that's something I will probably never have. And it's not some smug thing. It's a weakness.[35]

Therein lies the tragedy. Kobe says God put him on this earth to play basketball. I wouldn't argue that. He maxed out his talent and angels applaud that piece of his life, because God is a worker and wants us to exercise our gifts. But work became more than a means to an end, and it cost him the time needed to build friendships. Even his definition of a "good friend" isn't exactly the gold standard. Damn if our culture doesn't say, "Who cares! Look at all those championships! All that dough! The fame! The adoration!"

We all have the "obsessive" gene Kobe mentions. Maybe it's not a win-at-all-costs motor to be the best in our field. However, each of us has that *thing* we obsess over that takes us away from being others-focused. Maybe it's a desire for a relationship or the perfect physique. Often it's a past hurt we can't escape, so we obsess with booze, food, or sex to numb the pain. If we parse, then parse some more, what is the thing? Scripture says it's our broken relationship with God. The disconnect causes an unfillable emptiness which drives us to maniacal quests to fill the void. The Old Testament book of Ecclesiastes captures that obsession in the words of the wisest, richest man on the planet. Solomon lived large, explored all facets of human desires, and conquered everything a man can dream of to the point of making Wilt Chamberlain blush.

Are you a 2 a.m. friend? Nope, not the 2 a.m. friend you call when you're single and lookin' for a little hanky-panky. I'm referring to the friend you can count on who will talk you off the ledge. The one who will listen when it's inconvenient for their clock. The one who lives out these verses from John 15:12–14.

My command is this: Love each other as I have loved you. Greater love has no one than this: to

lay down one's life for one's friends. You are my
friends if you do what I command.

Verses like these cause the healthiest kind of wrestling. For one
thing, Christ states them as a command. He says we have to love
each other the way He loves us. For those who may not be fully on
board with this whole idea of Christ as Lord, the entirety of the
Bible paints an image of a God who loves us exponentially more
than we can fathom. However, instead of leaving the concept ab-
stract, He makes it ever so real, particularly for parents. He gives
up His one and only child for us. A very brass tacks gesture; the
weight of it is still difficult to grasp. Then He adds that we should
lay down our lives for our friends—in other words, sacrifice our
almighty agenda for the needs of our others. Would you? Hell, I
have nights I won't give up thirty minutes of Netflix when certain
names pop up on caller ID. It's tricky stuff, no doubt. When is it
legit to set boundaries? When is work genuinely more important
than taking the call of a friend who's hurting?

If the Bible is true, and I'm betting it is, then each of us will
stand in front of God. I try to err on the side that ensures the
Lord won't say, "Hey ML, great effort on knocking out that pre-
sentation for the client meeting back in July 2019. Glad you didn't
take the call of your buddy going through the divorce. Quarterly
earnings, Hulu, and lots of Instagram are what counts up here in
Heaven, Inc."

No, I'm gonna try my damndest to believe eternity is real,
where I'll have all the time I need to pursue dreams not yet con-
ceived. But on this side of heaven, I'm gonna fight to answer the
phone. It'll be messy, and in my selfishness I'll screw up often, but
hopefully I'll learn to relinquish my plans for the day and help you
live out yours—same as Christ did for all 7.6 billion of us.

Explore:

1) Do you get irritated when friends interrupt your day with a pressing personal matter?

2) Are you myopic with your career to the detriment of your friendships?

WEEK 19

I HAVE ANT POWER

*"A person who wields power cannot see truth; that is the
privilege of the powerless."* [36]

—*Lesslie Newbigin,* Foolishness to the Greeks:
The Gospel and Western Culture

I hate this statement: Christian theology says we're incapable of
managing our lives. We need our Creator and Lord to manage it
for us. The reason is that we're not nearly as smart or as powerful
as we think. The belief system goes a step further and says we need
a Savior. Please join me as I now place my fingers in my ears and
sing "La-la-la-la" while I tune out.

However, by tuning out, I show where my pride begins. It's
where my arrogance wrongly leads me down a path of futility.
Here are some verses that expand on the concept.

> This is the judgment, that the Light has come
> into the world, and men loved the darkness rather

than the Light, for their deeds were evil (John 3:19 NASB).

They do not know nor do they understand; They walk about in darkness; All the foundations of the earth are shaken (Psalm 82:5 NASB).

I form the light, and create darkness: I make peace, and create evil: I the LORD do all these things (Isaiah 45:7 NASB).

This is the brass tacks of how we show our hubris. We respond to these verses by saying, "That's not true. I'm managing fine on my own. I don't feel like I'm in the dark. I don't need Christ." And God gives us exactly what we ask. We march along and seek our own fulfillment and happiness, we vigorously pursue our agendas, and we don't realize the shiny "stuff" is not the best outcome. This is what God is referring to as "darkness." My close friends know my broken record joke: if you leave me to my own desires, you can bet your mortgage I'll end up in Vegas with a Scarface pile of coke and several women seeking payment for services rendered. Am I joking? Partially, but all of us have a dark side. And all of us can become immersed in accumulation and achievement as our end goal, as opposed to seeing all paths as means to help others. We also run into this ginormous problem known as death that hammers home our weakness.

I hate to admit it, but I recognize my deficiencies. There are thousands of things I can't do because they are not in my skill set. Collectively, here's a short list of humankind's inadequacies that validates Isaiah 45:7.

- We can't grow food.
- We can't generate rain.

- We can't manufacture the air we breathe.
- We can't create a child without help from the opposite sex.
- We can't control the finality of death.

Yes, we can grow crops, but I'm referring to the natural resources of planet earth. We assemble the parts given to us, but we can't create anything from scratch. In other words, ain't no one making seeds, dirt, and H_2O. The Isaiah 45 verse frames the conversation perfectly: God. Does. It. All.

I try to give perspective on this concept in my book *I'm Not Hitler* in relation to suffering, using ants as an analogy. Today I'll stick with "them bugs" to make a different point. Each person on Planet Earth can be equated to an ant in relation to genuine power. Like ants, we live in colonies. Those colonies are governed by a monarchy called a queen. There are soldiers who serve, protect, and gather food. Ant colonies have trails similar to roads that lead to other colonized villages, and some take up the equivalent of city blocks with several floors connected by walkways, like a multi-family high-rise. Yet for all that complexity and structure, a Joe Schmoe in brown socks can annihilate their entire city on a Sunday afternoon with a machine he purchased at Home Depot. On top of that, the dude who devastated the city is pretty much a larger version of an ant, living in his own city, serving, protecting, and gathering food. Said Schmoe is part of another 7.6 billion other ant peeps with very little influence, unless granted by the higher authority of God (Romans 13:1 NASB). The ant has limited influence on the lawnmower situation, and we're no different in relation to God's authority over the city, state, country, and world in which we live.

I'm not saying we're all worthless ants. We appear to be somewhat higher up the food chain, and maybe the argument is validated by God giving us superior cognitive abilities . . . at least compared to our little ant buddies. But don't get all high and mighty regarding your influence. We're limited in the grand scheme of things.

Psalm 88 below is an example of our powerlessness. It's known as the darkest psalm because it does not end with the usual rhythm of other psalms, where authors often remember how the Lord helped in the past or state their hope that He'll come through in the future. It concludes with darkness as the psalmist's only friend . . . and scene.

> LORD, you are the God who saves me;
>> day and night I cry out to you.
> May my prayer come before you;
>> turn your ear to my cry.
> I am overwhelmed with troubles
>> and my life draws near to death.
> I am counted among those who go down to the pit;
>> I am like one without strength.
> I am set apart with the dead,
>> like the slain who lie in the grave,
> whom you remember no more,
>> who are cut off from your care.
> You have put me in the lowest pit,
>> in the darkest depths.
> Your wrath lies heavily on me;
>> you have overwhelmed me with all your waves.
> You have taken from me my closest friends
>> and have made me repulsive to them.
> I am confined and cannot escape;
>> my eyes are dim with grief.

I call to you, LORD, every day;
    I spread out my hands to you.
Do you show your wonders to the dead?
    Do their spirits rise up and praise you?
Is your love declared in the grave,
    your faithfulness in Destruction?
Are your wonders known in the place of darkness,
    or your righteous deeds in the land of
    oblivion?
But I cry to you for help, LORD;
    in the morning my prayer comes before
    you.
Why, LORD, do you reject me
    and hide your face from me?
From my youth I have suffered and been close to
death;
    I have borne your terrors and am in despair.
Your wrath has swept over me;
    your terrors have destroyed me.
All day long they surround me like a flood;
    they have completely engulfed me.
You have taken from me friend and neighbor—
    darkness is my closest friend.

The writer is at his wit's end; he's desperate and crying out for help. Maybe his world was devastated by some version of the "lawnmower." I find verses six and eight fascinating in that the psalmist sees God as responsible for his desperate situation. While we're often culpable for decisions that get us in a pickle, the circumstances are part of a bigger plan way above our pay grade. I'm not referring to how people cherry-pick Jeremiah 29:11 and use it like

Mick Jagger did in "Far Away Eyes" ("Well the preacher kept right on saying that all I had to do was send ten dollars to the church of the Sacred Bleeding Heart of Jesus . . . next week they'd say my prayer on the radio and all my dreams would come true"). God's maneuverings always have an air of mystery; they're rarely binary. If they make sense all the time, the plans are likely our own small doodlings under our own agenda and not of the magnitude of what He can orchestrate in our lives.

Make no mistake; God sees us as more important and cares for us infinitely more than ants. The proof is that I've yet to come across an inch-tall dirt church with a teeny little savior on a cross.

Explore:

1) Has there been a time in your life where you felt powerless? What emotions did you experience?

2) Do you trust God's ability to reconcile all circumstances, regardless of whether they are due to choices you made?

WEEK 20

LIFE HAPPENS; WE WATCH

"Of two sisters, one is always the watcher,
one the dancer." [37]

—*Louise Glück,* Descending Figure

We rubberneck in traffic; we rubberneck in life.

Last weekend, I was sitting on my roof deck in Deep Ellum listening to the night. Car engines, motorcycles, laughter, and various white noise punctured the night as I enjoyed one of my favorite food groups: cigars. I peered at the high-rise next to mine, the Case building. I could see TVs in some of the windows, light flickering on the walls. There were people on balconies talking and laughing. Life was happening—some people living it and some watching it on TV. That's how we occupy time: we live life and watch life. Some of us want to chew it all up, live large, and feel all the emotions, whether high or low. Plenty of others stay hidden, not risking big joy or debilitating pain.

It's the same around the world. People scurry about, trying to love, live and work. Reminds me of driving through towns and villages in third-world countries where I'd see lights and TVs flickering in homes made of cardboard and aluminum flashing. They were also watching life and living life. Don't we all long to live and feel? I want to be in each room and engage, ask each person what's important? What are they thinking? What's inspiring? What's missing?

We're curious creatures; there's an inherent voyeurism to everything we do. Think of social media. We want to see what others are doing RIGHT. NOW. Wait ten minutes and check again—now what are they doing? We want to be where those people are. We wish we were on the beach with them or at the concert. "What if I missed the greatest show in the history of music?" Often, whether we admit or not, we want our lives to be like theirs. Or with television, we watch as a story unfolds. If it's a drama, we connect with the characters and their emotions. Maybe we want to live their big, cool adventure, their bravery, their sexiness.

That's where the longing begins, and the dysfunction. Maybe there is community being built online as we message or comment with friends on a particular topic, but it doesn't seem to compare to live engagement in person. Walking and laughing, sitting across from someone at dinner, looking at a person's face, in their eyes, sharing all the visceral dynamics: the sounds, the expressions, the smells, the flavors.

I guess that's the question: are we watching life to learn, or watching to escape? For me, when I watch a TV drama, whether it's a movie or a series, the story matters. I also feel the desire to escape. I want to shut my brain down and numb out a bit. We all need to decompress and rest, so I'm not saying TV is a gateway drug to evil and anarchy. But we sure do spend lots of time in front of that electronic device as it transmits other lives to us, same as our phones and computers. I feel the tangible anxiety when I watch food documentaries. Ones like *Mind of a Chef,* and others certainly connect with my adventuresome spirit. Right now I'm thinking of a little shack bar no more than ten feet by eight feet in Lomé, Togo, Africa. I'd never heard of the country until I went there with a fantastic organization called Mercy Ships. I remember sitting on one of five creaky wooden stools at night, a little dirt alley behind us, fifteen feet across, various folks strolling by with kiddos. You basically walk up to the wooden bar that's the size of a rectangular coffee table from the alley. One light bulb and a cooler on the ground. I remember looking at the moonlight, drinking a Castel, and thinking, *Man, this is pretty damn cool. I'm breathing African air and drinking a cold beer. Thank you, Lord.*

But the hunger doesn't stop. I want more. We're insatiable in our appetites for more experience, some of it a wonderful thing, lots of it an attempt to fill a void in our hearts. The scriptures below speak to being vigilant about not watching life go by, but making the most of our time.

> So, then, be careful how you live. Do not be unwise but wise, making the best use of your time because the times are evil. Therefore, do not be foolish, but understand what the Lord's will is (Ephesians 5:15–17 ISV).

> Our days may come to seventy years,
>   or eighty, if our strength endures;
> yet the best of them are but trouble and sorrow,
>   for they quickly pass, and we fly away.

> If only we knew the power of your anger!
>> Your wrath is as great as the fear that is
>> your due.
> Teach us to number our days,
>> that we may gain a heart of wisdom (Psalm
>> 90:10–12).

I try not to miss an opportunity to highlight how powerful scripture is. Pick anything you're struggling with at the moment—loneliness, addiction, anger, money, jealousy, lust, anxiety, worry, doubt—and scripture will address it in the form of a person. Never some esoteric, ambiguous cotton candy, but brass tracks truth that resonates from a real life story. The kind of words you can grab hold of and say, "I know the feeling." Sometimes the words are poetic; other times they're Hemingway-esque in their brute force. But don't kid yourself—this stuff isn't a bunch of fables for children. Biblical characters were flesh and blood like you and me, with the same damn battles and the same triumphs.

I do wonder, did they choose to watch life the way we do? I doubt it. Lord, teach us to number our days. Help us make sure we use your time given as a means to gain wisdom. Help us pursue important things in life and not shiny images on a screen.

Explore:

1) Where and when did you feel the most alive? Were you taking a risk outside of your comfort zone?
2) What thing or desire qualifies as insatiable for you? Does it feel manageable or out of control?

WEEK 21

DON'T CHEER FOR THE JACKASS

"Both men produced masterworks that millions have treasured. But readers finish Corbett's book feeling that both men had misspent their lives." [38]

—David Brooks, *"Do You Have to Be a Jerk To Be Great?"*

Does anything sting as much as the douchebag who succeeds? It seems we prefer the underdog over the cocky, despicable types, right?

In a rich op-ed piece in *The New York Times*, David Brooks asks the question "Do You Have to Be a Jerk to Be Great?" He pulls his content from two different books (one of which, *Range* by David Epstein, is waiting for me on my Kindle). The article is a quick read, and Brooks is always good. If you're not familiar with him, he's an expansive thinker and speaks as one of the moderate grown-ups in any room, whether cultural or political. He also references *You Must Change Your Life*, Rachel Corbett's biography of Auguste Rodin and his protégé, the poet Rainer Maria Rilke. The two had a singular focus and obsession with work, with Rodin telling Rilke "Travaillez, toujours travaillez" (work, always work).

As an artist—and *no*, I'm not claiming even a smidgen of the talent in Rodin's pinky toe—I do relate to the hunger to generate output while blocking out all the distractions of family and friends. Any time you hit a high watermark with your work or craft, it's as addictive as heroin. "Uh, yes please, I'll have another thousand hits." But Brooks speaks to the loss of real life—how we forfeit the stuff that matters when we choose to make work our ultimate goal.

Which leads to his headline question. It's a doozy we wrestle with (or I hope we do). Seems that some folks don't sweat being a jerk; as long as their hand ends with a royal flush, fuck everyone else. But most civil folks with a beating heart do feel the pendulum swing between insulated ambition and moral obligation to friends and neighbors.

If you're a Christ follower, there sure as hell better be tension. High-capacity leaders will fight the desire to let their ambition have its way, like a flooded river chewing up everything in its path. But the Gospels and pretty much all the rest of the New Testament speak to what's commonly referred to as the upside-down kingdom of God. In other words, the entirety of the New Testament (and much of the Old) not only encourages but *commands* us to surrender our agendas to a greater purpose of obedience and service. Yes, including the big career, bigger house, and cozy piña colada life. It's fascinating how even writing the word "obedience" makes me grit my teeth. And it's gender neutral—ain't none of us men or women jumping to the idea of bowing to a greater sumpin-sumpin than our passions. After all . . . I. HAVE. MY. DESTINY.

There is tension, from my experience. I've heard friends say "But this is business" as they refer to work as a separate bucket, immune to decency and fair treatment. Sometimes, if our work is directly related to sales or if we operate within a public company, there's a coldness, a "bottom line" mentality that separates us from the obligation to do the right thing. A win-at-all-costs ethos exists, which gets heightened when the outcome might affect our paycheck. This business reality gets very difficult when we see the jackass douchebags getting ahead—the ones who are completely self-focused and pretty much show their knives on the way up as they step on and backstab those in their way, or those lending a helping hand to others. Sounds like Rodin and Rilke fell prey to the same worldview; "They were both horrid to their wives and children."[39]

The psalmist below struggles with that tension. He sees the arrogant and shady folks getting ahead, and he damn near loses his sailor's legs: "my feet had almost slipped." He's been the good guy and feels like the Lone Ranger as others follow their own lead, living a carefree life with no consequences other than a fat time in Vegas.

> Surely God is good to Israel,
>> to those who are pure in heart.
> But as for me, my feet had almost slipped;
>> I had nearly lost my foothold.
> For I envied the arrogant
>> when I saw the prosperity of the wicked.
> They have no struggles;
>> their bodies are healthy and strong.

> They are free from common human burdens;
>> they are not plagued by human ills.
> Therefore pride is their necklace;
>> they clothe themselves with violence.
> From their callous hearts comes iniquity;
>> their evil imaginations have no limits.
> They scoff, and speak with malice;
>> with arrogance they threaten oppression.
> Their mouths lay claim to heaven,
>> and their tongues take possession of the
>> earth.
> Therefore their people turn to them
>> and drink up waters in abundance.
> They say, "How would God know?
>> Does the Most High know anything?"
> This is what the wicked are like—
>> always free of care, they go on amassing
>> wealth.
> Surely in vain I have kept my heart pure
>> and have washed my hands in innocence.
> All day long I have been afflicted,
>> and every morning brings new punish-
>> ments (Psalm 73:1–14).

You'll see how this psalm ends like many do, where the douche-bags are promised their comeuppance. Thankfully, according to Brooks' article, Epstein's data shows that some of us get to see the victory on this side of heaven. The generalists perform better than the specialists. Brooks captures it best in this sentence: "A life devoted to one thing is a stunted life, while a pluralistic life is an abundant one."[40]

Explore:

1) In what way(s) do you feel the most tension with seeing others get ahead who don't seem to deserve the success? In other words, what bothers you the most: their attitude or the feeling that you still have to play by the rules?

2) Do Psalm 73 and others provide comfort? Or do you find other ways to remain trustworthy of your circumstances?

WEEK 22

THE PSYCHOPATH IN ALL OF US

"That's why crazy people are so dangerous. You think they're nice until they're chaining you up in the garage." [41]

—*Michael Buckley,* The Fairy-Tale Detectives

I love to read. I also hate that I love to read. Why? Because I come across articles that send me into a spiral of worrying that I've lost my four remaining marbles.

In the Aeon article "Spot the Psychopath," Heidi Maibom, professor of philosophy at the University of Cincinnati, explores the nuanced personality of those diabolical creatures. Surprise, surprise . . . they're not much different than us. Maibom takes a measured and well-researched view; there's no sensationalized baloney. She has some gems, for sure, like this:

> They certainly aren't *incapable* of telling right from wrong, making good decisions or experiencing

empathy for other people. Instead, they suffer from a host of more mundane problems—such as being overly goal-fixated, fearless and selfish.[42]

Love that. Sounds just like me!

My first thought regarding psychopaths tends toward the Hollywood version, and Maibom covers this too: they "steal, lie and cheat, and have no respect for other people, social norms or the law. In some cases, they torture defenseless animals, assault other children or attempt to kill their siblings or parents."[43] But I knew she would turn the corner and paint a more vivid portrait that's parsed and complicated.

The nuance is what grabs me. We're black-belt Jedi Knights at placing ourselves on pedestals of moral high ground while looking down our Pinocchio noses at "those other bad people." The nice way of saying it is that we're unaware of our deficiencies. The sledgehammer version is we're liars. Scripture gives us the most comprehensive character study of people. To use modern vernacular, it says we're flawed, we make mistakes, and we can't control our big mouths.

All kinds of animals, birds, reptiles and sea creatures are being tamed and have been tamed by mankind, but no human being can tame the tongue. It is a restless evil, full of deadly poison (James 3:7–8).

Your tongue is not that bad? Maybe. But are your Facebook posts on presidential politics filled with Mr. Rogers "won't you be my neighbor" inspiration? Maybe at twenty-five years old, you haven't discovered the reality of your flaws, but I bet you're starting to notice some stuff. By forty? If you don't know the deep cracks in your armor, the tequila has pickled your brain. But we do try to mask it. "I'm not that bad . . . I pay my taxes . . . I haven't killed anyone." I cover this pride issue in depth in my first book, *I'm Not Hitler*. We kid ourselves by choosing the worst things in the world to compare ourselves to: murderers, rapists, sex traffickers . . . psychopaths. Well, gee, how damn easy is that? It's tough in our culture to be vulnerable and admit our insecurity, anger, jealousy, apathy, and general laziness. It's much easier to put on the mask and pretend to have it all together.

Here's where it gets cool. When you discover your flaws *and* admit them, it's the most liberating, joyous feeling in the world. There's nothing else to hide. When we stop trying to be perfect; when we admit to not having the answer during the client meeting; when we don't have to be right in the conversation; when we place the scary, dark thing out in the light? No, you won't martyr yourself with doom and gloom. Quite the opposite. Oh, man—life becomes a big ol' laugh. *The Gifts of Imperfection*, as Brené Brown calls them, will give you some serious hop in your step.

Which is why scripture is not a buzzkill rule book from a damning, meanie God. It's real-life stories of fractured people who need God to help them through life. It's a book where we see our broken selves and find hope in a God who provides a lifeline of freedom.

Explore:

1) Do you have any worries about being overly goal-fixated, selfish, and fearful of failure?
2) Are you comfortable and honest discussing your flaws with friends and mentors?

WEEK 23

PEACE, LOVE & DISTORTION

"I think perfection is ugly. Somewhere in the things humans make, I want to see scars, failure, disorder, distortion." [44]

—*Yohji Yamamoto*

August 14, 2019 was the fiftieth anniversary of Woodstock. The three-day festival has been dissected every which way over the decades, from the music to the politics to the reality and falsity of the ethos of the sixties. Netflix streamed *Woodstock: Three Days That Defined a Generation* as part of the anniversary.

What still bedazzles people is the ferocity of Jimi Hendrix's version of "The Star-Spangled Banner." It captures beauty, pain, war, chaos, and distortion. His rendition is polarizing. Plenty of folks are reverential of the power while another group despises the noise. There are glimmers of delicacy, hope, and inspiration. Like life, it's raw and amplified, guns and bombs bursting in air, sirens wailing, nights filled with screams, and deep, bellowing groans. Reminiscent of "This Is America" and played loud by a Black man who died too early at twenty-seven (something that happens often in our current climate), the song captures our cultural discord perfectly. America is divided; ain't many Democrats and Republicans chortling over their differences while buying another round. No, too often we're eviscerating each other with anger. Hendrix's sonic onslaught mirrors what scripture says about this world: there is beauty, love, and elegance, but it's mixed with lawlessness, war, and the piercing decay of morality.

Before we lump Hendrix into some hippy-dippy acid trip or dismiss him as an overwrought drug addict, remember that he enlisted in the Army and served with the 101st Airborne Division. His stint in the military gave him a unique perspective of both the military and civilian sides of the coin before he went on to incinerate the guitar landscape. The faces in the crowd at Woodstock were mesmerized (and possibly high), same as today when we hear this timeless masterpiece. The Whitney Houston version of "The Star-Spangled Banner" at the 1991 Super Bowl is extraordinary in its purity and inspiration, but it's too perfect for me. Hendrix's version captures the truth of life. We're messy, and in 2019, fifty years after he took the stage at Woodstock, people are still messy.

When we look back at the nostalgic pics of Woodstock, we realize it's not just an isolated moment in time. With Lollapalooza, Coachella, and Burning Man, every generation places their hope in music changing the world. The question is the same: can it? Of course! Nothing charms the soul the way thoughtful lyrics and harmonized instruments do. Today is no different. The same way Hendrix, The Who, and Ritchie Havens sang about freedom then, U2, Kendrick Lamar, and Childish Gambino are pushing their own version of freedom through rebellion now. Guess what? The original rebel pushing against "the man" keeping him down was that fella up there on the cross. Yep, Christ came and shook the earth one thousand times louder than Hendrix and his Marshall stacks. He gave a message to the establishment that still resonates today and will for all time. True love does exist, and there is no greater love than laying one's life down for one's friends (Jn 15:13). John Eldredge captures a version of Christ I prefer in *Beautiful Outlaw.*

> He is the playfulness of creation, scandal and utter goodness, the generosity of the ocean and the ferocity of a thunderstorm; he is cunning as a snake and gentle as a whisper; the gladness of sunshine and the humility of a thirty-mile walk by foot on a dirt road.[45]

Eldredge is right. Christ is amplified power. He's love at the highest level, more visceral than the hardest punch to the gut. However, when you first experience His love, you won't double over in pain; you'll fall to your knees in devotion.

Hendrix created four minutes of controlled anarchy that stretched boundaries for a generation of music fans. Christ brings a message of love that's disrupted billions of hearts for centuries past and future.

Explore:

1) We want music to change the world. Can you think of any music that has impacted lives at the level Christ has? In other words, has any song or band resonated for centuries?

2) Do you view the love of Christ as a powerful, amplified force? Or have you positioned Him as a passive, softer version of love with little impact?

WEEK 24

MY HONEST PRAYER

*"The great enemy of truth is very often not the lie—
deliberate, contrived, and dishonest—but the myth—
persistent, persuasive, and unrealistic."* [46]

—*President John F. Kennedy*

One of the top fifty iconic movie scenes is from *True Romance.* Dennis Hopper and Christopher Walken give an acting clinic in a face-off over how to tell if someone's spinning a yarn. The dialogue is classic Tarantino; his cadence leaps off the screen with these two acting legends.

I ask myself the question: how do I know when I'm lying? The fact is, it usually starts every morning at 6 a.m. over a cup of coffee and prayer. I lift up my pious thoughts and desires and put on my best mask—uh, face—of humility. I squint a little and give a gentle side-to-side shake of my head to help my earnestness. Sometimes I don a white robe, pull out the harp, and release white doves to fly free through my studio.

The more honest approach would be for me to drop the horse-shit and deliver this heartfelt message below to the Lord.

Father, You're welcome that I joined you this morning. I'm glad to give You my three minutes of half-hearted focus in the midst of fifteen minutes of drift. I'll read a devotional while thinking of my action items today, skipping over to Facebook and Instagram for a quick dopamine hit of envy. I pray You speak to me through scripture, even if I only see it on the big screen at church on Sundays. Speaking of, Lord, I'll give You an hour each Sunday . . . at the early service, so I don't miss the noon NFL game. I'll volunteer and serve others . . . maybe twice this year . . . for an hour at lunch . . . on Fridays. In December, if I make my bonus as planned, I'll tithe almost 2.5%, as long as it doesn't interfere with my vacation fund. After all, I worked hard for my money. I pray You help me spend two hours and twenty-two minutes on social media today. In return, You get five, maybe seven minutes in the evening, when I'm exhausted after binging *Game of Thrones* again. I'll pray for my friends for 2.5 seconds—You know the one, the impactful manifesto of "be with my friends." No name-dropping from me, because You know their specifics . . . plus, it would require another eight minutes of focus if I actually vocalized their needs. Thank You for this time I gave You, Lord. Remember my career goals and give me wisdom and strength to achieve all my desires. Amen.

Am I cynical? I think not. Best to show my true colors to the Lord. It's not as if He doesn't know them already, so why hide? My prayers are a disjointed mess. I have to focus intensely to make them remotely lucid. If not, the drift occurs after thirty seconds.

The most honest prayer I can fire up to God is one I stole from Anne Lamott, one of my favorite authors. If you're not familiar with her, she's sorta the female version of the humorist David Sedaris with a peppery sheen of Christ thrown on top. She's raw and laugh-out-loud funny as she probes the depths of sorrow and heartache, like in this gem: "You can safely assume that you've created God in your own image when it turns out that God hates all the same people you do."[47]

Her prayer is " 'Help me, help me, help me,' and 'Thank you, thank you, thank you.' "[48] Boom. Amen. The rest is pretty much splitting hairs, right? I guess you could start with the "thank yous" first and then do the "helps," but God is already a thousand moves ahead in hearing our pain. "In the same way, the Spirit helps us in our weakness. We do not know what we ought to pray for, but the Spirit himself intercedes for us through wordless groans" (Rom. 8:26).

The best prayer I can come up with sounds like this.

> Lord, thank You for putting up with my selfish ass. Thank You for sticking with me 24/7, year after year, when I look to You so rarely. Please teach me to give You all of my life, the way You did for mankind. Even a smidgen of Your sacrifice would make me a better man. Help me reverse my twenty-four hours; instead of one for You and twenty-three for me, flip it. Make me sacrificial. Make me a good listener when friends speak. Fewer words, more ears. Help me remember that my agenda isn't as

important as I think. Help me lose my ego-driven goals and adopt the needs of others.

Help me, help me . . . thank you, thank you. In Christ's name. Amen.

Explore:

1) Have you ever prayed for longer than two minutes? Try praying for five days straight in the morning with no phone or computer. Notice anything different after those five days?

2) Can you determine what issues stop you from sincere prayer? Have you created unrealistic expectations for the outcomes?

Week 25

WHEN WORLDVIEWS COLLIDE

"There's a culture in the U.S. where children are showered with encouragement. So everyone who grows up in the U.S. is overconfident. We need to use our wisdom to guide them and help them. Because we are better than them." [49]

—Jeff Lui, President, Fuyao

I recently came across a riveting documentary, *American Factory*, about how Chinese-based company Fuyao invested in and retooled a closed General Motors plant. Roughly 2,000 Chinese team members relocated to work with American hires. I anticipated a retread of the challenges of unions versus bottom-line efficiency or automation forcing companies to dismiss factory workers. Instead, the story focuses on well-intentioned people ramming into deep-seeded cultural issues.

As the story unfolds at the plant in Dayton, Ohio, we peer into deeply rooted worldviews related to work, comfort, country, pride, idolatry, and servitude. The Chinese are company and country first. To them, the billionaire owner of the Fuyao company is the leader, spoken and bowed to with deep reverence. Production and efficiency are key, with quality of life a distant placeholder behind twelve-hour days and few, if any, holidays. The American workers are just grateful to have jobs, thought they're not as well paid as they were at GM, and want favorable working conditions—a fair requirement. However, having worked at General Motors immediately after high school, I remember an air of entitlement with the union workers. The desire teetered on comfort first, value and profitability second. The fact that the the Fuyao factory was made possible by a 2008 GM plant closing speaks to the harsh global competition that every country faces. The forces of capitalism are designed for profit, and if efficient and cheap labor helps, so be it, cozy workplace be damned.

That's the key element for me: are both sides equally wrong or right? The Chinese appear to be comfortable with a lifestyle of all work and little play. I mean, who wouldn't be motivated by dancing pixies in the film singing these lyrics at the corporate party: "May the best come, may the worst leave . . . Intelligence and lean manufacturing . . . All industries should adopt them . . . Finance, service, manufacturing . . . Intelligence and lean manufacturing . . . Technology is developing rapidly . . . The Information Age has already arrived . . . Employee relation system is amazing . . . Great at resource integration and market response."[50] Yes, catchy and memorable, said no one ever.

I can't help but think, though, that the American position is also wrong. There's an air of pride; a wee bit of "don't push us too hard because we're more fragile than the auto glass we make." And woo doggie, does the Jeff Liu quote above hit a nerve. He speaks toward the end of the film as frustrations are rising and the Chinese management team is seeing the American gaps that need to be filled. How dare he speak such truth about us? We're 'Mercans, dammit! Ah, but he's right. We are told from a young age that we can do anything we want—pursue and achieve our dreams. Walk into that room like you own it! We can't help but reek of hubris when everyone gets a ribbon, no matter what place they finish. That's why we're so offended when we go to France and they have the insolence to *not* have ice in their water! I may picket at La Madeleine tonight on principle alone.

The documentary reminded me of an excellent post I read on the most famous thorn in the history of mankind. The article "Why You Have That Thorn" is from the *Desiring God* blog. The writer, Jon Bloom, touches on how we hate the idea of being weakened for our own good. God gives us a thorn (or thorns) like He gave to Paul in 2 Corinthians 12 to keep our almighty egos in check. The theology is fascinating, but I'll stick with the topic at hand in relation to America and China, or any country with a significant GDP. Our pride for our counties, and more importantly, for ourselves, is what gets us in trouble. EVERY. TIME. It often begins with "I deserve (fill in the blank)," a thing or status you really don't deserve because where did we get that idea in the first place?

> Pride, in all its manifestations, is our most pervasive sin and the most dangerous to us spiritually. Anything God gives us to keep us humble and prayerfully dependent on him is a great gift—even when that gift causes us pain.[51]

This reminded me of the viral clip of Stephen Colbert and Anderson Cooper where Colbert, in a most tender gesture, mentions that the death of his father was a gift and beautifully unwraps the "why?" His worldview starts from the Christian ethos that this life will include suffering (as Christ suffered for us) as a means to get us to our real life, the eternal one after we pass from here. We don't deserve 24/7 bunnies and sunshine; we don't deserve happiness. But to own this reality, you have to adopt a worldview that is not Chinese, not American, not even of this world to begin with.

The fact is, our pride is a massive barrier to remembering that our very existence is a gift. In other words, we ain't got nothin' to do with the begat. I didn't choose me, make me, or birth me. I happened because the Lord willed it. Nope, it wasn't science. Science is not a thing-maker, as many atheists and agnostics want to believe. Science is the study of the things being made. Our postmodern culture has pushed hard—with extensive pride—to remove intelligent design (God) from the equation and funnel the massiveness of God as the ultimate Artist, Creator, and Engineer into small vials of measurement with no brain, agency, or purpose. How prideful is it to think that every machine, computer, tool, clothing item, plate, cabinet—every item you see in your home—was clearly designed by engineers, technologists, carpenters, and machinists, but we humans, the beings who designed all that stuff . . . naw, we came from mud. A big explosion created us with no strategy and no brain—only millions of years as the sole variable. How arrogant for us to lay claim as to where the totem pole ends.

I can make productivity and country my idol. I can also define my life by a posture of entitlement. Or I can choose to recognize the highest authority of Christ as the true President and CEO of all things, including all the joy and pain in my life.

Explore:

1) Can you identify the idols in your life? Here's a hint: what are the things you feel you can't live without?
2) Has pride impacted you in the past? Why does God speak so negatively about pride?

WEEK 26

DON'T STEP ON MY
FABERGÉ EGG

*"Surely it is the one who fears he is wrong who avoids
criticism. The one who is sure he is right invites it. It only
illuminates the strength of beliefs and makes them more
available to others."* [52]

—*David L. Wolfe,* Epistemology: The Justification
of Belief

I learned a new phrase recently: "White Male Fragility." A friend
taught it to me and said it's all the rage in the counseling world
(yes, she's a counselor). *Oh, cool,* I thought. *I'm already digging the
sound of it.* She forwarded me an op-ed piece by Rex Huppke titled
"Column: Bret Stephens, Donald Trump and the Epidemic of
Male Fragility" that delves deeper. The piece centers on David
Karpf, an associate professor of media and public affairs at
George Washington University, who tweeted that Bret Stephens
was a "bedbug." You can read the rest, but there's a whole other

tangent of how something minor can catch fire and burn down the media house.

The issue revolves around our insecurities—a weakness—not to be mistaken for vulnerability—a sign of strength. We get all outta sorts over the slightest affront (and even that's too strong a word). As Huppke touches on, we demand apologies for teeny little hangnails of disagreements. There's a difference between character assassination and slander when it comes to public figures being disagreed with oe someone using sarcasm to make a point.

It's a minefield, for sure, and intent, intelligence, and nuance impact the outcome. Words do matter, and legitimate issues such as #MeToo should keep us vigilant about how we use our words. However, being too cautious can make us tepid and half-hearted with our positions, which ultimately affects the truth.

This reminds me of a good friend I had lunch with not too long ago. He often texts me and says, "You ain't Black because [insert Black culture reference]." Yes, he's Black. This results in a slew of back-and-forth, with me saying things like, "Naw, I'm Blacker than you because [insert another Black culture reference]." What concerns me is how often I hesitate to use this example. "Uh-oh . . . what if someone misreads these texts and misjudges me and thinks I'm insensitive or racist?" Boom. I feel timidity rising in a bad way. The fact is, he and I have rich conversations because we ask questions with education (and ball-busting humor) as the goal. He knows my heart and I know his. We're brothers who end each encounter with a hug and a "Love you, man," like I do with many men who sharpen and inspire me. Keep in mind, this is where nuance and intelligence play a role: I've earned those conversations with him. There's nothing worse than a dopey white guy stepping out of his lane and saying something racially insensitive, or something misogynistic to a woman. As always, it's a heart issue. If my intent is to cause pain or get a thrill with my words, then my heart is busted and in need of repair. I have plenty of thoughts about how comedians feel it's their right to offend people with a joke because "Hey, man, it's all in jest," but those are words for another day. But if I take a position that contradicts another person's idea, does that make me insensitive? Is their ego—whether white, Black, male, or female—too fragile? Or am I bulldozing a point with no regard for the recipient, which is essentially another form of insecurity masking a need to win? Those are some stormy seas to navigate for sure. As a Christ follower, I hold positions deemed offensive to a secular world. While I've developed a thick skin when discussing matters of faith, I for damn sure have my dainty little places drenched in ego. They're innocuous in the grand scheme of things, but if I hear or receive something wrong, I may see it as an affront to my eggshell fortitude.

Huppke sums up the solution well with this insight below, which could be said another way: lead with humility, don't be a bully, and apologize fast.

> This isn't hard, fellas. Don't punch down, don't overreact, admit when you've made a mistake, listen to other people and learn from them and stop acting like you're the only one in the world whose feelings matter.[53]

Jesus adds another layer to the mix with the scripture below. Taking a position for Christ places a person in the crosshairs. Not only are you saying that Christ stands for a *version* of truth, you're saying He *is* truth.

> You will be hated by everyone because of me, but the one who stands firm to the end will be saved (Matthew 10:22).

Will my fragile little weenie ego deny Christ in the face of scrutiny? What if I offend my family and friends by not only standing for my belief in Him but encouraging them to jump on the train? Woo doggie, there's some 800-pound tension. If I care deeply about my friends who don't care to know about Christ but I believe fervently in His saving grace, how can I not broach the subject? Yes, it will often offend people. If Christ is truth, the pronouncement will sting to hear, no matter how nuanced. Hell, it pummels me at times when I rebel against Him.

Can I balance my delicate insecurities with the withering assault I invite by believing in and sharing faith in Christ? I guess I'll find my fortitude when I stop checking how many people have unsubscribed from my blog.

Explore:

1) Are you afraid to speak truth to your friends because you worry about disappointing them?
2) Do you get offended easily? Is there an insecurity you need to address?

WEEK 27

GRIEF IS A WILD ANIMAL

*"The darker the night, the brighter the stars,
the deeper the grief, the closer is God!"* [54]

—*attributed to Russian poet Apollon Maykov*

We've all felt nausea hit us out of nowhere. Like a wave washing over us, we feel the symptoms immediately. Grief is similar, but with a more powerful punch. It can double us over, take our knees out, and leave us wordless and heaving deep sighs.

In two separate articles I've read, the writers describe grief as a force of nature, almost animalistic, with an uncontrollable wildness to it. In "10 Years without Steve," *Dallas Morning News* op-ed contributor Tyra Damm discusses the emotions she's felt in the aftermath of her husband's passing. Elizabeth Gilbert, the author of *Eat, Pray, Love*, also touched on the subject in a TED podcast with Chris Anderson. In the interview, she says:

[Grief] happens upon you. It's bigger than you. There's a humility that you have to step into, where you surrender to being moved through the landscape of grief by grief itself. And it has its own time frame, it has its own itinerary with you, it has its own power over you, and it will come when it comes. And when it comes, it's a bow down, it's a carve out . . .

There are certain things that happen to you as a human being that you cannot control or command that will come to you at really inconvenient times and where you have to bow in the human humility to the fact that there's something running through you that's bigger than you.[55]

We have to bow down to a force greater than ourselves. In the piece on grief above and in her TED video, Gilbert recognizes that there's something outside of us steering the ship. I'm fascinated by how people describe the force of grief when they recognize it as the greater power in the equation. Many folks refer to this entity as "the universe," which seems so cold and lifeless, particularly in relation to grief. When Gilbert or Damm speak of "things that happen to you as a human being that you cannot control or command," I do understand why someone might view the experience as a universal force. Upheaval in our lives often seems random—it certainly seems unfair and out of bounds. A multitude of *whys* flood our thoughts. If there is a loving God we view as a Father who cares about us so deeply, why does He allow so much tragedy and pain?

This is where Gilbert and Damm may have a different perspective. In the *Dallas Morning News* piece, Damm mentions leaving her longtime church for a new congregation. While the relentless pain from losing someone is the same for both women, the suffering might be viewed differently through Christian goggles. A cold, dark universe doesn't provide a solution to the hurt, to the incessant cries of "Why?" Christianity offers hope in the form of a man who suffered greatly and died an unfair death. This person of flesh and blood shares our grief when He asks the Father, "My God, my God, why have you forsaken me?" (Matt. 27:46).

That's a God I can hold on to during the trials of life. He understands pain, being betrayed by friends, and upheaval in a chaotic world. The story of His life recounts the struggles of countless hurting souls, desperate and wondering if God has hung up the phone. In Psalms, I can read about people with emotions that sound reminiscent of Gilbert's. I can shake my fist at a physical being who understands; after all, He lived it. Grief brings such a sledgehammer of emotions that I can't imagine crying out, "Oh universe, oh science, oh evolution, why have you left me here?"

Gilbert says, in another powerful statement about grief:

> I have learned that Grief is a force of energy that cannot be controlled or predicted. It comes and goes on its own schedule. Grief does not obey your plans, or your wishes. Grief will do whatever it wants to you, whenever it wants to. In that regard, Grief has a lot in common with Love.[56]

For me, the word "love" can be substituted with "God" in that final sentence. That's the God I worship. He can't be tamed. He doesn't follow my calendar. No matter how many times I rub the lamp, He doesn't grant my wishes 24/7. Yes, I believe He's the origin of all things, both good and bad. I have to fight to trust that God is a beast of love, and on this side of heaven, He often delivers love in vehicles filled with pain. I don't like it, but I trust He has reasons beyond my reasoning and for my good.

Explore:

1) When you deal with grief, what or who is your foundation to help you through the pain?
2) Are you able to place your trust in God when life is hurling grenades at you?

WEEK 28

MY LOVE LANGUAGE IS PAIN

*"You think your pain and your heartbreak are
unprecedented in the history of the world, but then you
read. It was Dostoevsky and Dickens who taught me that
the things that tormented me most were the very things that
connected me with all the people who were alive, or who had
ever been alive."* [57]

—James Baldwin

I've told my community group that God's love language often feels like He punches me in the nose and says, "Trust me, it's how I show love and it's good for ya!" Uh, thank you . . . and . . . praise God?

The book *The 5 Love Languages: The Secret to Love that Lasts* by Gary Chapman is a perennial best seller because it speaks to how we best give and receive love in our relationships. Chapman says the five love languages are:

- receiving gifts,
- quality time,
- words of affirmation,
- acts of service, and
- physical touch.

He left off a sixth theological love language called "getting the everlasting shit kicked out of you." Can I get an amen? By far, this is one of the biggest struggles for secularists and religious folk alike when it comes to believing in and trusting God. In other words, it's the classic question, "Why do bad things happen to good people?"

This is a follow-up to the previous chapter, "Grief Is a Wild Animal." A good friend and mentor read it and was concerned that people would misread it and see God as the harbinger of both good and bad. In other words, does God give us pain in the form of cancer, a tragic car accident, or a spouse who cheats? The answer is one for the millennium and never easy to process. On this side of heaven, if I had a wife and punched her in the nose and said, "Babe, trust me, this is what's best, you'll understand someday," that relationship wouldn't be perceived as one of devoted love. Yet the divine Lord of the universe does appear to deliver seasons of hurt that can last much longer than a black eye. He does seem to be the abusive lover who tortures us at times.

The fact is, He's not. The most difficult thing for our finite minds to comprehend is why a sovereign God allows pain to occur. Yes, I know it feels like splitting hairs. What's the difference between delivering and allowing pain? The theological reality is 1) the world is broken from original sin way back with those crazy Adam and Eve kids, 2) there is an enemy whose sole purpose is to wreak havoc, and 3) people are born with an inherent cancer known as sin. I don't like the word "sin" because it's become a bastardized word in our culture. However, the fact is, you do make mistakes—my preferred word choice. Often, those mistakes are blatant and egregious, and afterwards you feel overwhelming guilt and a need to apologize. That's another way of describing sin.

Back to theology. Bigger brains at much higher pay grades have wrestled with why God allows evil and pain in our lives. It appears utterly random, it's always disruptive, and it creates a woozy set of sailor's legs when it comes to trusting that the Lord has our best interests at heart. May I simply say out loud, it is absolutely okay to doubt, to question, and, yes, to be disappointed in God. We're human, and pretending to play the good little Christian who praises God on the outside when a slew of f-bombs are brewing inside sets you up for an eggshell relationship with Him.

What I've personally experienced with loss and disappointment is a deeper sense of life and a more lucid understanding of my limits. It's what James Baldwin says above in the quote: pain helps us understand and empathize with others in a way that winning and happiness can't touch. God knows that for us to be fully formed people, we need all the emotions played out in a lifetime, including the soul-sucking hurt we want to avoid. Life can't be a constant uptick to the right. The gravity of pain does enrich us in the long run, as much as we hate it in the short term. Read Psalms or Job and allow yourself to shake your fist at things that don't make sense. Two books I recommend are *The Problem of Pain* by C. S. Lewis and *If God Is Good* by Randy Alcorn. Neither are a walk in the park, but both answer tough questions of how a loving God can and will knit together a beautiful tapestry out of bloody knots. Neverland won't happen in this lifetime; God didn't plan it that way. I'm sorry we have to experience pain and grief, but I also trust that, in the midst of doubts, the Lord will reconcile all the hurt.

Explore:

1) Have you had seasons of disappointment and pain where you then saw positive lessons on the other side?

2) Do you find yourself being sucked into the Western mindset of "everyone deserves the white picket fence of success?"

WEEK 29

GIVE BECAUSE YOU DESERVE EL ZILCHO

"Man is not, by nature, deserving of all that he wants. When we think that we are automatically entitled to something, that is when we start walking all over others to get it." [58]

—*Criss Jami,* Diotima, Battery, Electric Personality

I applaud the work of Park Cities Baptist Church in Dallas, Texas. For the past eighteen years, they've made a commitment to helping people living in the rural "colonias" on the outskirts of McAllen, Edinburg, and Pharr, Texas. The PCBC team builds and distributes beds and does basic construction on homes chosen by two rock star Hispanic pastors dedicated to helping their communities. These colonias are in some of the poorest zip codes in the United States. The residents are stuck in a desperate cycle of poverty that zaps all hope for a better life. I got back to Disneyland (Dallas) on

Saturday night after a short, four-day trip to the colonias with the PCBC team.

The trip got me thinking about a verse in John 12:8. Jesus says, "You will always have the poor among you, but you will not always have me." He gives no additional context, there's no parable to unwrap, and there's almost a flippant feeling of *que sera, sera* . . . and scene. But I knew there had to be more, so I went online to find insight on the verse. Turns out Christ was referencing verses from the Old Testament and likely testing His audience to see how well they had listened to their rabbis' teachings.

> If among you, one of your brothers should become poor, in any of your towns within your land that the LORD your God is giving you, you shall not harden your heart or shut your hand against your poor brother, but you shall open your hand to him and lend him sufficient for his need, whatever it may be. For there will never cease to be poor in the land. Therefore I command you, "You shall open wide your hand to your brother, to the needy and to the poor, in your land" (Deuteronomy 15:7–8, 11 ESV).

Not much to expand on regarding that directive. It's a command to help those in need. There's no grey area or wiggle room for us to assess whether the person *deserves* help or not. I've also struggled to find the verses that say, "Feel free to do this only when convenient." Dammit.

For me to understand these verses, I had to lose big, watch dreams die a slow death, and have my plans disrupted continuously. I had to be put on the mat with no way to get up. When I found myself broke—again—no matter how well I planned or how efficiently I executed those plans and the bank account continued to be negative, then verses like the ones in Deuteronomy began to resonate. In other words, I hadn't come to the end of myself. I still thought I was savvy and tenacious enough to muscle over the mountains. I perceived "me" as the master of my universe, able to control the chess moves of my life. Trust me, you'll know when that freeing moment happens. It's scary but oh, so liberating to realize that God controls your provision or that health is another power play by the Lord. The best place a person can land is in the absolute recognition of his or her place in the pecking order of life. The resulting outcome will be a big dose of humble pie and newfound empathy for others' struggles. You'll pass judgment less often, and you'll listen well and be the ambassador of grace the Lord wants you to be.

Every person reading this chapter has to decide how much scripture they believe. Spoiler alert: you won't find any verses that say, "Cherry-pick what works for your definition of truth and kick to the curb the verses that challenge you." In other words, the Bible wasn't written for us to say we like maybe 50% of it, give or take. In poker vernacular, scripture is "all in." Let me preface by saying if you would've met me a week before Friday, October 22, 1999, I would've told you all of scripture was complete bullshit and I didn't understand why adults insisted on believing in the tooth fairy. On that date, God grabbed me in a metaphorical headlock and said, "Look here, young buck. You ain't all that." He provided a proper ass-kicking in a loving way and informed me of who's in charge of all things truth.

The most common pushback I hear from people who do not believe in Christianity is the fact that the Bible was written by people. The idea is that people are fallible and untrustworthy, so how can we base our reality on a 3,400-year-old document that was likely fabricated? Sometimes the statement is said with humility and genuine struggle, which I have plenty of grace for. Often, though it's said in a sort of "gotcha" way, like a big reveal has occurred. When someone uses that tone, I fire back, "Ask tougher questions. All the scholars at the top seminaries and universities in the country are very aware. You haven't cracked some secret code no one knew."

If you're dismissive of the text, my challenge for you is to disprove the Bible. A big chunk of people around the world with very large brains have wrestled deeply, asked all the tough questions, and decided (with God helping to shed light) that the document is true down to every last tittle. You'd need to bring a mountain of evidence to disprove this timeless book. It doesn't allow room for people to say, "Good for you, ML, but I've got my own spirituality." You have to create a bigger truth that disproves the Bible and Christ that's more than a flimsy opinion. As I've mentioned in the past, when you do empirically prove the content is false, you will, without a doubt, be the most famous person in the history of the world, bar none.

This brings us back to having to decide whether the Deuteronomy scripture is what we have to believe and live out. I could just as easily be poor and homeless; it's only by the grace and mercy of the Lord that I'm not. Since my vaunted talent, tenacity, and ego have nothing to do with my position or the roof over my head, I for damn sure better have open hands and give to those in need. They deserve to have my stuff because my stuff wasn't mine in the first place. The Lord provided it, and I deserve el zilcho.

Explore:

1) Are you aware of your powerlessness in the grand scheme of things? Or do you feel capable of controlling your world?

2) In the United States, it's difficult to not feel entitlement. What does scripture say about what we deserve?

WEEK 30

WHAT'S YOUR PURPOSE?

"The best things in life make you sweaty."

—*author unknown*

Whoever said the above quote is on point. When done right, dancing, a mosh pit, spicy food, and shenanigans between the sheets must include some sweat. The same is true of work. Physical labor requires elbow grease, which leads to a feeling of completeness—a good day's work. The same goes for intellectual sweat; when a solid strategy is implemented and well executed or a client pitch is nailed, the cerebral horsepower required is a form of mental sweat.

In the three-part Netflix documentary *Inside Bill's Brain: Decoding Bill Gates*, we see one of the wealthiest men on the planet making his second act a legacy that may stand the test of time. I've been unable to think of another titan of industry who has taken his or her formidable fortune and steered it toward tackling the most serious problems on the planet. He uses not only his own wealth but that of other billionaires as he recruits them to join The Giving Pledge. Imagine if you had that brain capacity plus an almost infinite treasure chest at your disposal. Add in unmatched tenacity, and diseases like polio can be eradicated. Issues such as sanitation and clean water become problems to be attacked instead unsolvable puzzles that make us throw our hands up in hopelessness.

From the outside, it sounds easy to hop off the "Dominate-Technology-Make-Billions" train and sit back on the beach with a piña colada. But anyone with a smidgen of ambition and an understanding of the human condition knows it's our nature to say, "More, more, MORE!" Plus, to have the unbridled boldness and intellectual ability to build an empire like Microsoft? It's the same as asking Mick Jagger why he continues jumping around onstage after fifty years of touring. Engines like that are built to motor until they die. But Gates has made the shift. Maybe due to the influence of his wife, Melinda, he's decided to use his superpowers for good. Wow, is it fun to watch how he and his wife are leveraging their resources with other brilliant minds to impact millions of people.

One option when watching the documentary is to check out and say, "Hell, I'll never have his options. No need to even try to make a difference." But that'd be easy and a form of cowardice. Yes, the definition of cowardice is "lack of courage or firmness of purpose."[59] Each of us have a purpose, and it's likely not as an Instagram influencer or a contestant on *America's Got Talent*. Do you think about purpose? In your twenties, the question seems easier because the runway appears long. But damned if that clock doesn't tick-tock fast. We end up grasping at The Flash. "Did something just fly past me!?" Yes, that would be your life.

Before I get all Bible-ish on you, let's look at the practical benefits of seeking purpose. For one, it will include work. Work is a good thing, not to be avoided or dreaded. Yes, it's often arduous, but same as exercise, it's designed to build muscle in the form of responsibility, character, and humility. Purpose should also include impact on others. Yes, in the form of being courteous, respectful, and empathetic. I'll make the argument without scripture that a life of purpose must also include some level of service to your fellow humans beyond kind gestures of decency. Purpose should include sacrifice, right? If not, purpose distorts into myopic ambition of self.

At the same time, I recognize that when life kicks, and when circumstances appear unchanged, we feel hopeless and question whether there's any significance to each day. In other words, purpose becomes tertiary to survival. Thankfully, we have a God who understands battle fatigue. After all, He questioned His purpose and sweated blood when thinking of the outcome in Luke 22:44. "And being in anguish, he prayed more earnestly, and his sweat was like drops of blood falling to the ground." This is where I *love* me some scripture and nerding out on apologetics. Dave Miller, a Ph.D., clarifies this passage in the Gospel of Luke (Luke was a physician).

> Only Luke referred to Jesus' sweat (*idros*)—a much used medical term. And only Luke referred to Jesus' sweat as consisting of great drops of blood (*thromboi haimatos*)—a medical condition alluded to by both Aristotle and Theophrastus. The Greek term *thromboi* (from which we get thrombus, thrombin, et. al.) refers to clots of blood. . . .
> We can conclude quite justifiably that the terminology used by the gospel writer to refer to the severe mental distress experienced by Jesus was

intended to be taken literally, i.e., that the sweat of Jesus became bloody. A thorough search of the medical literature demonstrates that such a condition, while admittedly rare, does occur in humans. Commonly referred to as hematidrosis or hemohidrosis, this condition results in the excretion of blood or blood pigment in the sweat. Under conditions of great emotional stress, tiny capillaries in the sweat glands can rupture, thus mixing blood with perspiration.[60]

Gates's sweat will impact millions of lives for generations; Christ's blood has saved billions of hearts over centuries. Finding your purpose will include sweat, and if the stakes are high enough, to steal a great movie title, there will be blood in the process. What if your sacrifice results in a singular objective that changes one, ten, or a hundred lives? I'm not being syrupy; we can generate purposeful desire with tangible outcomes in a snap. My friend Chris Bailey works a job, raises a family, cheers for the Rangers, and impacts thousands of homeless friends every year by organizing toy, sock, and sleeping bag drives via his grassroots campaign, Everybody Love Everybody. He doesn't need billions of dollars—only a realization that a life of purpose requires a choice to sweat for others.

Explore:

1) When you think of your purpose, how much do your goals include service to others?
2) What simple steps can you take to move toward a greater purpose? Start with writing out your goals, and then work backwards on what needs to be done to achieve them. Start small; make them reasoned and doable.

WEEK 31

THEATER OF LIFE

"The real issue is there's one billion people overeating, and one billion people that don't have access to food." [61]

—*Chef Alain Ducasse*

When living in Disneyland—I mean, Dallas—or any major metropolitan city, we can't help but think that everyone has seventeen options of olives and fifty-seven versions of balsamic vinegar at their local grocer. We forget—or may not be aware—that things like food deserts exist, even in Big D. (Side note: check out the awesome work of Bonton Farms.)

I love me some documentaries, and one that grabbed me on Netflix is *Theater of Life*. It highlights a passionate chef who's doing his version of Bill and Melinda Gates's The Giving Pledge. Chef Massimo Bottura encourages his fellow world-renowned chef buddies to eliminate food waste by cooking gourmet meals for the less fortunate. They've made their personal marks as restaurant elites, and now he's pushing them to make a difference for those who will rarely step foot in a Michelin-rated destination. It has plenty of piercing "feelz" and warm fuzzies while illuminating the reality that every country has a population of folks struggling to survive each day. Roughly three-quarters of the way through, the quote above from Chef Alain Ducasse leapt off the screen. What hits me like a brick is the idea of a billion people overeating juxtaposed against those who don't have access to food at all. Those kinds of numbers put me on my heels, but I hate resting in hopelessness or apathy.

The numbers remind me of a similar statistic directly in my backyard. The North Texas Food Bank provides incredible data points like this one: "In our 13-county service area alone, nearly 800,000 neighbors live in food-insecure households, and this includes 300,000 children."[62] That's an interesting way to phrase it—*food insecure*—and likely a more compelling way of communicating hunger pains. Austin Street Center has a similar statement that will stick with me until the grave: "Homeless people experience *relational poverty*"[63] (emphasis mine). When life turns upside-down, those two distresses go hand-in-hand: people don't have food, and they don't have people. Most of us rarely experience a lack of either, and if we do, it's only a trigger to go out with friends and enjoy dinner.

What comes to mind is a C. S. Lewis quote. If you're not familiar with him, I mention him often. He's one of those dead guys who says all the best things, sorta like a theological Mark Twain or Winston Churchill.

> If you read history you will find that the Christians who did most for the present world were just those who thought most of the next. . . . It is since Christians have largely ceased to think of the other

world that they have become so ineffective in this.
Aim at Heaven and you will get Earth "thrown
in": aim at earth and you will get neither.[64]

I'll try to connect the dots between an Italian chef and a British
theologian who's been dead for over fifty years. I have no idea
whether Massimo Bottura is a Christ follower, but he's very much
exhibiting Christlike qualities by feeding thousands. He's looking
outward and impacting people in need. In other words, he's living
out what us Jesus freaks refer to as "kingdom vision." He's exhibiting attributes that are not the norm in this world. What Lewis is
saying is the more we think about eternity—a place that lasts forever—the less we'll focus on the less valuable items of this world
that are temporary and irrelevant.

Yes, I hear your pushback. "I don't need Jesus to be a giving person." Yep, you're right, you don't. But please run this little
experiment: spend a year volunteering twice a month and donat-
ing about $500 a month to a charity. I purposely picked excessive
sacrifices of time and money because most of us don't give either.
Then spend a year, twice a month, excessively shopping, drinking, lounging on the beach, going to Vegas, doing lunches at the
club, spending $500 a month on you alone, and not doing anything
sacrificial for others. Pay attention to the endorphin high you get
when you're serving compared to what you get in your time of
self-indulgence. See if you feel better when you get everything you
want or when you give little moments of joy to others while making sacrifices. Maybe a way to measure it is to add up the "thank
yous" you receive versus the receipts you accumulate—then tell
me how you feel.

The point I'm making is that God has wired us to serve; therefore, we feel better as people when we help others. And who gave

more than any person in the history of mankind? Jesus Christ. John 1:1–4 says,

> In the beginning was the Word, and the Word was with God, and the Word was God. He was with God in the beginning. Through him all things were made; without him nothing was made that has been made. In him was life, and that life was the light of all mankind.

Those verses are saying that Christ was there in the beginning. When time began; when the universe started; when atoms, molecules, and every scientific thingy big-banged; He snapped His fingers to make it so. He is the originator of all stuff, including the desire to help and the associated dopamine hit we feel. Yes, please do challenge that assertion; please wrestle deeply with the concept of Christ as the origin of service to others.

Hell, I was moved by simply *watching* someone help others on Netflix. Imagine if I got off the couch! At the end of the day, isn't that we want—to have a life full of meaning? To feel satisfied with how we score each day? Wouldn't we rather have tangible metrics of sacrifice beyond a saccharine Instagram or Facebook meme of "Live your best life?"

So what do we do? First off, I'll continue to encourage you to get down to a local food bank and help. They make it eazy-peezy for a person or group to show up and roll up their sleeves. Make the time to do it; the dividends for the food bank are exponential, but the effect on your worldview will be profound.

Regarding the idea of eternity and heaven, I again glean from Lewis in Mere Christianity:

Most of us find it very difficult to want "Heaven" at all—except in so far as "Heaven" means meeting again our friends who have died. One reason for this difficulty is that we have not been trained: our whole education tends to fix our minds on this world. Another reason is that when the real want for Heaven is present in us, we do not recognize it. Most people, if they had really learned to look into their own hearts, would know that they do want, and want acutely, something that cannot be had in this world. There are all sorts of things in this world that offer to give it to you, but they never quite keep their promise.[65]

I love how Lewis mentions the struggle of betting on an ambiguous heaven. "Uh, what is it exactly? Can't see it, touch it, hear it or smell it, so I'm gonna focus on what's tangible." A quick refresher on Lewis: he was an Oxford scholar and atheist who set out to prove that God didn't exist. In that journey, he discovered not only God but God in the person of Jesus Christ. He's pushing us to think of heaven because the logic is sound: eternity is forever and our time here is vapor. If it's true, then separate the wheat from the chaff with what's empty in this world and the next.

After you begin serving, buy an ESV Study Bible. Start asking questions about eternity. Read the overviews and introductions to the various books in the Old Testament and New Testament. Study for ten minutes each morning while sipping a cup o' joe.

At the very least, you'll begin to have a balanced life of work, play, and service, and maybe the three will get reversed. You may also be surprised to find that a new relationship will open up with that JC fella and profoundly change your heart, mind, and soul.

Explore:

1) What can you do today to schedule a time of service to those in need?

2) If eternity truly lasts forever, shouldn't our primary goal be to ensure all our family and friends get there?

WEEK 32

GRUDGES VS. FORGIVENESS

"Not forgiving is like drinking rat poison and then waiting for the rat to die." [66]

—*Anne Lamott,* Traveling Mercies

There may be no better barometer of soul stability than rush-hour traffic. One day, I was driving to an early morning Bible study while navigating 75-Central. Spoiler alert: waving a middle finger or muttering "What is this jackass doing?" are sure signs that unrest rules your heart.

Upon arrival to my group, gentle greetings followed by prayer completely settled me and changed my mood from foul to to upbeat. That got me thinking about anger, resentment, and grudges. Not that I struggle . . . just asking for a friend.

It seems the human condition consists of grudges. We sure like to hold 'em. When I check my anxiety levels and do a deep-dive of my triggers, there's often a feeling of "I've been wronged," which, at its core, is an unruly need to feel in charge and be right.

The simmering rage is usually over the most ticky-tack of stuff—maybe a guy at the gym not saying "pardon me" when he accidentally bumped my shoulder. Thankfully, there are other freaks I can point to who have much bigger issues than I do (he says, dripping with sarcasm). I read an article in *Medium* about a guy who kept a list of people who had wronged him, and even had a scoring system. I'd like to think I'm above that, but the only difference is I'm not keeping a tactile ledger. Mine are upstairs in the noggin, and I've caught myself rehearsing zippy comebacks to crush my opponent . . . sort of like De Niro in *Taxi Driver*, but, of course, much more Mensa-esque and passive-aggressive like.

There's little argument that holding grudges is woefully toxic to our system. My body displays tangible evidence of holding the grudge. There's fatigue, irritation, and lack of focus. Compare the difference between letting loose with one of those witty barbs versus when you ask forgiveness. In the former, a sense of guilt occurs, particularly when you can see the hurt in someone's eyes. With the latter, a wave of relief washes over you, like an angelic validation from the heavens. The fact is, angels may be applauding (1 Peter 1:12 NIV).

The brilliance of scripture is that it speaks to all our foibles. There are several verses specific to how our grudges, when voiced, are caustic. There are plenty of others that speak to the reality that God is trying to protect us from ourselves. James 3:6 is a brutal indictment. Do a word study in scripture on the word "tongue." The imagery is vivid and positions the muscular organ as a thing capable of poetic beauty or, if not contained, a weapon of extreme violence.

> The tongue also is a fire, a world of evil among the
> parts of the body. It corrupts the whole body, sets

the whole course of one's life on fire, and is itself set on fire by hell (James 3:6 NIV).

Keep your tongue from evil and your lips from speaking deceit (Psalm 34:13 NASB).

Your tongue plots destruction, like a sharp razor, you worker of deceit (Psalm 52:2 ESV).

Set a guard, O LORD, over my mouth; keep watch over the door of my lips! (Psalm 141:3 ESV).

Forgiveness—more powerful than anger, resentment, and grudges combined—is at the heart of Christianity. Often, we get lost in the weeds, thinking the Bible is a rule book designed to kill our buzz. Quite the opposite. That feeling of relief and healthy satisfaction from offering or asking for forgiveness is another sign of how God has wired us. We, like Christ, can forgive others, and we can also forgive ourselves. Of course, not at His level, but when bringing His grace into the mix, the outcomes are revelatory. Colossians 3:13 pretty much says it all:

> Bear with each other and forgive one another if any
> of you has a grievance against someone. Forgive as
> the Lord forgave you.

Verses like the ones in Colossians pack a wallop. They force us to process deep theology. "Who is this man who claims to forgive all sins? How does that work in the grand scheme of things? More importantly, what does that look like with my friends, my family, my coworkers, and the folks driving next to me on the highway?"

Lord, take away all grudges. Help me forgive as You forgive a couple billion times a day.

Explore:

1) Are you able to forgive easily or do you hold grudges?
2) Is there someone you're currently angry with who you need to forgive? Try reaching out and forgiving them, whether they own the wrong or not.

WEEK 33

THE MYSTERY OF THE TIPPING POINT

"Look at the world around you. It may seem like an immovable, implacable place. It is not. With the slightest push—in just the right place—it can be tipped." [67]

—*Malcolm Gladwell,* The Tipping Point

A tipping point is such a fun concept—the thing, event, or circumstance that causes a product, business, or pandemic to scale. I'm a big fan of pretty much all of Gladwell's books. He gets beat up by lots of folks for having less-than-empirical evidence, but I think the dismissal is cloaked envy of his success. His anecdotal style is compelling, and hey, I'm fine wearing a simpleton T-shirt. Plus, even the best empirical evidence is doused with some pixie dust. In other words, no one can nail down the exact formula of what makes something go bananas in sales. Check out Dan Ariely's *Predictably Irrational* as a good read on how kooky we are.

My question: who's ultimately responsible for the tipping?

In one episode of Reid Hoffman's podcast *Masters of Scale*, he interviews Tory Burch, and they discuss company culture, when to scale fast, and when to be patient. In all his interviews, there's an inherent curiosity about the special sauce that guarantees magic. *Masters of Scale* is always compelling and produced at a high level, and Hoffman has a fantastic voice, capturing hunger and passion. Plus, as a gazillionaire (cofounder of LinkedIn and venture capital firm Greylock Partners), he understands the entrepreneurial personality and still speaks "startup." In the podcast, Burch mentions her tipping point of success: what's known as the "Oprah moment." Oprah's producers invited Burch to be on Oprah's show after a PR friend of Burch's (unbeknownst to Burch) sent Oprah some of her clothing line for Christmas. While this was a strategic move, trust me—Oprah probably had multiple warehouses of products from hopeful entrepreneurs who wanted to surprise her audience with coffee mugs that double as salt and pepper shakers.

On the other side of the pendulum swing is one of the best-selling devotionals of all time: Oswald Chambers's *My Utmost for His Highest.* It's been one of my go-to devotionals for twenty years as a Christ follower. Why is he on the opposite swing of the pendulum? For several fascinating reasons that lead to my main point. Oswald died at the age of forty-three in 1917, well before we had coolio ad spends and viral marketing campaigns. In addition, he didn't publish the devotional; his widow, Biddy Chambers, did after his death by cobbling together his notes and sermons. Sales are estimated at around $13 million, and the paperback has never been out of print since Biddy first had it published in 1927.

One of my personal peccadilloes is when successful people paint a grandiose image of their workmanlike tenacity and ability to see around corners as the variables that drove their meteoric accomplishment. Please hear me, yes yes yes . . . any triumph must have stains of blood and sweat, plus a gifted intellectual arsenal. However, there's a huge amount of mystery to what catapults a TV show like *Seinfeld* or four lads from Liverpool or a social network like Facebook. Ever heard of Friendster, Ringo, Google's Orkut, or Tribe? One option for the cause of the tipping is to assume sheer force of personality. But that falls flat with Oswald's widow. I've found no account of her as a Molly Brown-esque hurricane. How in the hell could she orchestrate such scale over decades? Another choice for the mystery is an ambiguous "universe" dispersing planets, Martians, and good luck charms. A third choice is to look to the Lord as the chessmaster of all things large and small. While that is my default position, I wrestle often with the idea that God is the engineer of all the machinations. I also have to remember I am the ant in this equation and look past my pride of perceived intellect.

The beauty of scripture is that it speaks to God's unfathomable expanse and His intimate involvement in the details. Check out the verses below alluding to His enormity and finesse. Here's what I love about the complexity of the Bible. Work, commerce, and business are not excluded from the narrative. The verses below are directly applicable to the twists, setbacks, and pivots of Tory Burch and Oswald Chambers. In other words, God *does* open the door to Oprah or keep a book in publication for over ninety years—or even 2,000 years.

> Yours, O LORD, is the greatness and the power and the glory and the victory and the majesty, for all that is in the heavens and in the earth is yours. Yours is the kingdom, O LORD, and you are exalted as head above all (1 Chronicles 29:11 ESV).

The heart of man plans his way, but the LORD establishes his steps (Proverbs 16:9 ESV).

Are not two sparrows sold for a penny? And not one of them will fall to the ground apart from your Father. But even the hairs of your head are all numbered (Matthew 10:29–30 ESV).

Cool. Do we all join hands and close in prayer? On some days, yes, I can hold the tension with a monster dose of ambiguity glue. Other days, the mystery is overwhelming—particularly when disruptive tragedy strikes. I throw up my hands and think, *For fuck's sake, how do you expect me to trust that there's any level of clarity here? You allow genocide, yet also keep up with my shaved head?* I again have to lean into scripture and find verses like Romans 11:36 (ESV): "For from Him and through Him and to Him are all things. To him be glory forever. Amen." Then I have to meet other Christ followers here and around the world—all in agreement that within the mystery of tipping points and tragedy, we can find trust.

Explore:

1) Do you feel you are the ultimate driver of circumstances in your life? In other words, do tipping points occur based on your actions?
2) Can you hold the tension of God holding the entire expanse of the universe in His hand and your tiny life on Planet Earth?

WEEK 34

I NEED HEAVENLY COCAINE

*"You may not feel outstandingly robust, but if you are an
average-sized adult you will contain within your modest frame
no less than 7 x 1018 joules of potential energy—enough
to explode with the force of thirty very large hydrogen bombs,
assuming you knew how to liberate it and really wished to
make a point."* [68]

—*Bill Bryson,* A Short History of Nearly Everything

As an entrepreneur, I regularly have business ideas percolating.
Some come and go in a day and others fester. Today, I'm think-
ing the next big thing is 72-Hour Energy. Yessir, only weenies
drink that sissy 5-Hour stuff. The new sheriff in town is 72-Hour
Energy, sort of a "meth lite." Tagline: "Live Your Best Inner
Tweaker."

If only I could maintain a healthy energy level. In my quest for
Deep Ellum and world domination, I've become a Jedi espresso
shotmaster. Every morning, I have a cup of coffee with an espresso

shot, followed by a second cup of coffee. After lunch, when I feel
Mr. Food Coma tapping my shoulder, BAM! I shoot back a couple
more espresso shots.

At the core of this exercise is a desire to stay crisp, be rigorous with work, and stay on top of things. Even the thought of a
ten-minute power nap has me racing back to the espresso machine
for more magic elixir to stay electrified. A casual glance at grocery
store shelves filled with fifty different energy drink options shows
that we seem to be chasing a high or fighting an epidemic of sleep
deprivation. The fact is, we feel the need to go, go, go. For sure,
I could blather down a tangent about FOMO, but I've discussed
that at length in my first book. This content is about the fatigue
of life.

These nefarious energy thoughts were triggered when I
read a Facebook post from a writer friend that elegantly captures how I feel many days. She is a Christ follower, so her goggles are tilted toward the idea of good and evil on the spiritual
front. Though it's not necessary to believe in that—although
you would be smart to do so—you can read this post from a
posture of "life is hard" or "the universe isn't delivering as I'd
hoped."

I know you are exhausted from the battle.
I know you're afraid things will never change.
I know you are ready to give up and walk away.
I know you're deep in resentment for being put in
this position.
I know you feel ill-equipped for the battle.
I know this isn't how you wanted things to be.
I know it feels like God has abandoned you.
I know you feel alone.[69]

When reading the lines, there's a deep sigh from the weariness of her truth, but also relief in realizing I'm not a freak. There's at least one other person who has similar thoughts swirling around upstairs. Yes, there's another series of questions of whether I or she should (or could) fix those circumstances. Maybe; maybe not. We live in a culture that doesn't like the idea of stillness, of exploring thoughts of doubt. This is 'Merca. We gotta live our best life; a loving God would never place me in a position of not being happy. Staying static is unhealthy and I. Must. Change. This.

One of the toughest theological lessons to comprehend and own is the idea that God sometimes allows or orchestrates a dog-shit year (or years) for us while keeping His long vision. The both-and is that often, we're the purveyors of the shit-storm; we're the culprit who got ourselves in the pickle. Regardless of who engineered the circumstance, the desired outcome is to drive us to the verses below.

> May the God of hope fill you with all joy and peace as you trust in him, so that you may overflow with hope by the power of the Holy Spirit (Romans 15:13).

> Do not be anxious about anything, but in every situation, by prayer and petition, with thanksgiving, present your requests to God. And the peace of God, which transcends all understanding, will guard your hearts and your minds in Christ Jesus (Philippians 4:6–7).

Here's the challenge. Can I live out those verses? On some days, yes—the power of prayer, scripture, and the Lord's grace at work in me have that exact effect and there's no need for thirteen espresso shots. There is a peace that transcends all understanding, and it's not found in nature, on the beach, or in hot yoga. It requires effort and a calculated surrender and admission that I am not the God of my universe. The irony of it all is that I have the best chance of feeling this peace when things are not going as I'd hoped. Why? Because when the good stuff happens, it's far too easy to congratulate Mike Lyon for his boldness. After all, Mike Lyon is so capable and influential that he refers to himself as The Mike Lyon.

The Lord wants us to realize that He is the ultimate energy drink. He tells the woman at the well in John 4:13–14, "Everyone who drinks this water will be thirsty again, but whoever drinks the water I give them will never thirst. Indeed, the water I give them will become in them a spring of water welling up to eternal life." Yessir, I can tweak on that all life long.

Explore:

1) If you feel low-level or even high-level anxiety about stretching every hour of each day, can you pinpoint the exact issue of why you don't trust God with your days?

2) Are you able to trust what the Romans and Philippians verses say about God giving you peace and trust? If not, what do you need to surrender to Him?

WEEK 35

IT'S JUST A JOKE

"You have to know how to be vulgar.
Paint with four-letter words." [70]

—*Pablo Picasso*

Art is perceived in a thousand ways depending on the viewer's frame of reference, worldview, and even family of origin. I remember after college when I was making a living as a visual artist. I had several influences, but Picasso was one of the first who knocked me on my ass. His blue period still gives me goosebumps, as does plenty of his cubism. One man's masterpiece is another's ignorance. I remember my dad looking at a coffee-table book I'd purchased of Picasso's unfathomable body of work and saying, "Anybody could do that." God love him, I wish I could say he was drunk, but I'll chalk it up as a naive understanding of genius.

That's a long windup to say my take on the Picasso quote is be reckless on the canvas and in life. Break rules, don't be safe, and make a bold statement, and possibly maybe, you'll end up in the history books.

Comedians have a similar mindset. The craft of extracting laughter from an audience consists of abrupt changes in direction from the expected. We laugh because the artist surprised us with his or her verbal dexterity. There's a fine line between laughter and jaw-dropping shock, and the masters toe the line at daredevil heights. From my vantage point, there's no artistic endeavor as brave as stand-up comedy. A theater actor is often part of an ensemble and the environment is established as a passive audience receiving the performance. A band has each other, and even a solo musician has an instrument as a bodyguard. Think about it: all a comedian has for protection from the drunken hordes is their vocabulary and a mic. Maybe they have a prop or two, like Carrot Top and Gallagher do, but the real game is played with words alone.

Dave Chappelle, Sarah Silverman, Amy Schumer, and Chris Rock are, I'd say, the current Mount Rushmore of the raunch, and I'm a fan of all of them. They built their foundations on groundbreakers such as Richard Pryor, Joan Rivers, and Redd Foxx. I would watch videos of Richard Pryor for hours. His cadence and rhythms were matchless—still are. There's also a long list of clean comics such as Jay Leno, Jerry Seinfeld, and Ellen DeGeneres, and I have mighty respect for their discipline.

The question I'm posing for the day is this: can a comedian go too far? Let me state up front that I'm a big fan of all of the comedians listed above. Their timing and their ability to weave a yarn and turn on a dime is awe-inspiring. But I often find myself laughing and cringing while watching. There's a level of guilt I feel, as if my mom caught me with my hand in the cookie jar before dinner. The standard rebuttal I hear from all comics is the laugh is all that matters. In other words, there is no line to cross except one of silence. My inner barometer disagrees. For clarity, I'm not wandering down a freedom-of-speech debate. Censorship isn't a win. We need the bad to measure when comedy bits—or tweets—digress to slander and character assassination.

I was relieved when I found out I'm not quite the old guy in brown socks yelling at those crazy kids to turn down their devilish rock 'n' roll. Plenty of critics feel that Chappelle crossed the line in *Sticks and Stones*. In a CNBC article, the writer said, "Many of the jokes were perceived as tone-deaf and hurtful, particularly those which used various groups of people as punchlines, such as women, sexual assault victims, Asians and members of the LGBTQ community—transgender people in particular."[71] "Ah, come on sweetie, but I made you laugh" is how most comedians default.

We must turn to something beyond the zeitgeist to test our spirits. Let's wrestle with one of the most provocative statements in the history of mankind from John 1:1.

> In the beginning was the Word, and the Word was with God, and the Word was God.

And scene. What this means—flatly and forcefully—is that words do matter. Specifically, there's one Word that matters most, and it has authority over all other words, sentences, documents, and books. Yes, that'd be the Bible. We turn to God's Word as the final jurisdiction on all matters, even above the Constitution. I encourage you to wrestle with that concept and try to dismiss scripture as a centuries-old version of the telephone game or kick it to the curb and try your best as a good person without an absolute litmus test to measure against what's good enough.

Let's take things a step further to set the foundation of authority. In Genesis 1, the God of the universe spoke things into existence.

And God said, "Let there be light," and there was light (v. 3).

And God said, "Let there be a vault between the waters to separate water from water" (v. 6).

And God said, "Let the water under the sky be gathered to one place, and let dry ground appear" (v. 9).

Then God said, "Let the land produce vegetation: seed-bearing plants and trees on the land that bear fruit with seed in it, according to their various kinds" (v. 11).

And God said, "Let the land produce living creatures according to their kinds: the livestock, the creatures that move along the ground, and the wild animals, each according to its kind" (v. 24).

Then God said, "Let us make mankind in our image, in our likeness, so that they may rule over the fish in the sea and the birds in the sky, over the livestock and all the wild animals, and over all the creatures that move along the ground" (v. 26).

In other words, the Grand Poobah above all others gave an order, and water, light, dirt, air, flesh, and blood said "yessir" and hopped.

Did this all happen in seven days? Not likely by our clocks, but for damn sure it wasn't a brainless jackass named evolution working alone in a void.

When I notice these inner turmoils stirring from any content I'm absorbing, I ask myself, *what's happening in my spirit?* On the musical side, I have to be cognizant of my frame of mind when listening to Zero 7, Radiohead, or Massive Attack. I love 'em, but there's a tonality that can send me to a dark place. I need the same diligence when listening to comedians, or any cultural leader, for that matter. I have to turn to the official Word again for verses like these:

> Do not let any unwholesome talk come out of your mouths, but only what is helpful for building others up according to their needs, that it may benefit those who listen (Ephesians 4:29).

> So encourage each other and build each other up, just as you are already doing (1 Thessalonians 5:11 NLT).

I'm not saying you must cover your ears from all things curse word. After all, a targeted f-bomb serves a purpose. Each person has to make their own assessment of when and how their compass gets pulled off track. Maybe the question before that is what do you use as your guide? If it's not scripture, it's something. Your mind is a sponge absorbing data for sixteen hours a day, and statistically that data comes from social media, Hulu, Netflix, and Amazon Prime.

We'd all be smart to discern what's our line, who determines it, and how much we can tippy-toe up to or over it. As you do, remember to pepper your Chappelle, Schumer, and Rock with the timelessness of Christ.

Explore:

1) Have you experienced a time where you realized that words do matter? Something you wish you could take back, or a time you stepped over a line?
2) Is there something other than the Bible you use as final authority for where the line is regarding truth and opinion?

WEEK 36

ARE YOU AWAKE?

"People who don't believe are walking dead.
They are asleep." [72]

—*Kanye West*

"When was the last time a gospel record was number one on the Billboard 200?" a good friend asked. A great point, as the media and fans bat around whether Kanye is now officially batshit crazy or has simply experienced an awakening of faith.

James Corden interviewed West on one of his wonderful karaoke segments, this time Airpool Karaoke with Kanye West. There's a longer, twenty-minute segment, but the shorter, four-minute cut captures the meat of the discussion. For one, Corden sounds like plenty of folks: "You actually read the Bible?" Secondly, I love Kanye's metaphor about being awake or asleep. Or is it a fact?

One of the many reasons the Kanye story is so brilliant is that he's such a polarizing figure, exactly like the man-God in whom he now claims to believe. Yes, I do sense sincerity. I also think he'll continue making mistakes, like all of us fallible folks, Christ followers or not. Will that make me doubt him if he falls off the Jesus wagon and falls prey to a vice like booze, porn, drugs, or . . . pick your poison? Not at all. He simply reflects our collective need for the gospel. The other thing that came to mind is this: here's a guy who's reached the pinnacle of the world: fame, fortune, worshiping fans, plus babe on arm. But from the sounds of it, he was miserable and has now found some level of bliss. Fascinating how Christ consistently delivers the magic.

As always, we have the choice of writing Kanye off as a celebrity kook. What about those joyous gospel singers on the plane? Are they kooks too? That's the arena where I love to pick fights. I recently had a conversation with an atheist friend who holds the position that we 2.1 billion Christians are delusional. I'm open to the idea and state it repeatedly in my first book: we may have fallen for the biggest hoax and scandal in the history of mankind. I don't equate mass numbers of followers as a sign of veracity; groupthink doesn't prove anything. However, a consistent narrative of dramatic heart, mind, and soul change does add weight to the evidence.

What I long for is the atheist who will come to the table and be open to the idea that he or she might also be delusional. Possibly, maybe Christ is exactly who He claims to be in the most historically validated book ever written and agnostics, atheists, and those of other faiths have missed the boat. Yes, in some ways, that's a tough truth, or it might be a crystal clear, singular path. In my friend's case, he said no, it's only us Jesus folks who are hallucinating. That idea is disingenuous at best and outright jack-assery at worst.

Kanye will likely lose lots of fans as much as he will gain others. For non-Bible readers, even the original King Himself had to deal with "fans" walking away. We often forget that, even with Christ performing miracle after miracle in living color, He still had people not drinking the grace Kool-Aid. If I were Him, I would've riffed, "Sheesh, tough crowd . . . raise people from the dead, cure the blind, heal lepers, what else can I do here? I'm outta rabbits. Actually, wait for it . . . I have one more big one."

A friend posted this on Facebook from a devotional, and it felt apropos to Kanye's discussion with Corden.

> The best reason to give your life to Jesus Christ is because you need Him. You need Him for this life, and you need Him for the life to come. So far in life—whether you realize it or not—you have been following the devil. He promised to give you happiness and peace. But has he kept his promise? No, not at all—nor will he ever keep it. He also promises that you don't need to worry about what will happen to you when you die—which is another lie.[73]

What I love about that excerpt is that it has all the hocus pocus that secularists hate—all the God-and-devil whackadoo stuff. However, it also touches on a reality that has caught my attention lately (or, as Kanye would say, that God has placed on my heart): YOU ARE GOING TO DIE. When we try to dismiss the stone cold fact of this life, I'm astonished at the hubris some people display. How can we not give serious consideration to something that is inescapable? If someone tells me that 100% of the oxygen in my room is leaving in twenty-four hours, do I sit back and grab another beer? Only a moron would not look for a solution. Therefore, logic tells me people have fallen for the lie in the last sentence of the excerpt. They assume they'll be all peachy when they die, as if Willy Wonka will automatically give them a golden ticket to the afterlife based on merit.

The Bible is such a rich book because it's not brimming with bunnies and sunshine. It speaks to how plenty of folks won't believe, and I empathize. Twenty years ago, I was adamant in my position that Christianity was for ninnies, which is why I understand my atheist friend's dismissal.

Jesus answered them, "I told you, and you do not believe; the works that I do in My Father's name, these testify of Me" (John 10:25 NASB).

Some were being persuaded by the things spoken, but others would not believe (Acts 28:24 NASB).

Was I skeptical when I first heard about Kanye's conversion? Yep—the same as I was with Justin Bieber, or with Charlie Sheen, if anyone recalls his dalliance with Christ before his tiger blood gave him all the juju he needed. Hell, I'm skeptical of my own conversion on some days. However, Kanye's story has too many of the signs, and it's the consistent story I've heard from people I've met around the world. There's a peace to him in the four-minute clip with Corden, a twinkle of comfort that he knows he's found spiritual gold.

Explore:

1) When Kanye says most people are asleep in life, would you agree? What are they missing?
2) Do you have any fear of the afterlife? Do you give any thought to the idea of heaven?

WEEK 37

MY DOMINANT DESIRE

"Increasingly, Americans are people who believe in nothing, and care for nothing, and seek to know nothing, and interfere with nothing, and enjoy nothing, and hate nothing, and find purpose in nothing, and they live for nothing, and they only stay alive because there's nothing worth dying for." [74]

—*Gary Brandenburg, "A Crash Course on Happiness"*

"What's your five-year plan?" I remember being a young twenty-something, and that was a common question when contemplating the future. If the question came up in an interview, I would conjure up my best blather: "I want to continue growing as a person and be in a career where I help the team, build value for the company, and rise to a position where I can help others achieve their goals . . . oh, and save all the children in the world . . . and build snowmen for those in need . . . and, uh, provide puppies for the children I don't save."

I have to relinquish the sarcasm and admit that some folks do live out the hockey-stick uptick, or at least a general 10–20%

return on investment on "life wins." Life simply works for them. However, I know far too many others whose five-year plans went up in flames, and the various subsidiary pivots resulted in loss of more teeth and blood. Often, as life kicks us over and over again, plans and dreams turn into questions of how not to drown in despair, each day one of survival. I remember going to my ten-year high school reunion and already seeing cracks in the armor. Yes, there were plenty of folks "peacocking" about their perfect spouses, careers, and Mensa-scoring three-year-olds. But there were others where I could see the spark fading already. Five years later, at a spur-of-the-moment fifteen-year reunion, I started to hear about the divorces and the tragic deaths of lives cut short. The challenge of nothingness was beginning to blossom.

Brandenburg's conclusion may be accurate; or, at best, we misplace our desires in a hard-charging career, binging on Netflix (guilty), molding perfect children, or scrolling away two to three hours of social media each day. Maybe it's living for the weekends, checking things off the bucket list, or pulling for your favorite pro team to win a title. Please hear me: none of these things are inherently bad. The question is whether they are *the* dominant things that rule your thoughts. Personally, I fight regular battles against wanting work and achievement to be my measure of value, as well as battles against the nuanced emotion of affirmation, people-pleasing, and apathy toward hard truth. I have to evaluate my dominant thoughts throughout the day. We all have them; it's a question of what occupies our minds. As a Christ follower, the easy answer is "I think of Jesus 24/7 . . ." And swoon. Nope, that would be a bullshit answer. Yes, I do contemplate and wrestle with Christ throughout my day, but it's a messy gumbo for sure. Those righteous thoughts are intermittent. As a single, heterosexual dude, there are numerous tangents of sexual desire, misplaced ambition, and passive-aggressive scorekeeping, then a smidgen of prayer, followed by more sexual desire. And that's before breakfast.

At this stage of life, I do my best to run the big thoughts, debates, and decisions through a biblical worldview. I take the temperature of everything, whether relevant to me or others, and ask, "What does scripture have to say?" Which segues back to pastor Gary Brandenburg's incisive statement above. For damn sure there are plenty of folks waking, working, and striving for the good life where, at some stage, they can retire, travel, golf, and frolic and fritter about. But as I once heard at a men's luncheon, "Good luck finding verses in the Bible about retirement."

The sledgehammer question for all of us is this: are we going to pursue purpose to the point of dying for a cause? I can't say I know for certain that every person must stand for something to the point of death. Maybe? If I were a teacher, could I, should I, would I die for the cause of education? No: I think my example is misdirected. The question seems to be this: what is *the* most important thing in this brief snap of a life? That's where I find clarity in the biblical worldview. Maybe a teacher educates his or her students and the underlying foundation is peppered with a Christian ethos. No, not forcing scripture on the students, but endearing an attitude that plants curiosity in faith for the students. The same could be true for a banker, a chef, or a postal worker. In Philippians 2:3–4, the apostle Paul says,

> Do nothing out of selfish ambition or vain conceit. Rather, in humility value others above yourselves, not looking to your own interests but each of you to the interests of the others.

I'd prefer to dismiss those verses and say, "Naw, I'm not interested. That Paul guy sounds like some manner of super religious guy. Me, I got real-world responsibilities. I'm no professional Christian." Then I have to wrestle with this teeny little verse in 1 Corinthians 11:1, causing me to grit my teeth.

Follow my example, as I follow the example of Christ.

I have to make a decision of how much of that there Bible I believe. I have to evaluate whether the content is for a select few—like that Paul guy—but not for me in 2020. Can I dismiss the content as not relevant to contemporary life? Are there verses that give me an out, that give root to the idea of not spending my days pointing people toward Christ? Dammit . . . I wish I could tell you there's an entire book in the Old Testament or New Testament that encourages a life filled with Vegas, sushi, and cigars. Actually, there is one. Check out the book of Ecclesiastes, and especially 12:13 for his conclusion after a life of indulgence:

> Now all has been heard;
>   here is the conclusion of the matter:
> Fear God and keep his commandments,
>   for this is the duty of all mankind.

More gritting of teeth. In *I'm Not Hitler,* I have a chapter titled "Who's the REAL Boss?" In other words, do I have the authority to dismiss the contents of scripture as irrelevant to me? It's the same question Brandenburg asked in his sermon, and it's forty-five minutes of worthy listening. Any time we choose to disagree with Christ, we have to weigh our authority in the equation. In other words, will people dismiss the teachings of Christ in favor of your contradictory position? Maybe for a moment, but a century from now, your authority won't hold salt. Bank on it. Fast forward 2,000 years to the year 4019, and Christ's authority will still usurp all others. He won't be forgotten.

If you make the decision to make Christ your dominant thought, there's a 100% money-back guarantee you won't have to worry about nothing creeping into your life.

Explore:

1) What are your dominant thoughts each day? Are they positive or negative?

2) When it comes to belief in the Bible, do you believe all of it, some of it, or none of it? Do you have the authority to dismiss it as false?

WEEK 38

BAD AS ME

"If you're not the most sinful person you know, you don't know yourself very well." [75]

—Jeff Warren

I'll find any reason to reference Tom Waits, Rock and Roll Hall of Fame inductee, voice polished with bourbon and broken glass. Few can turn a phrase like him. He's worth an hour on YouTube watching his interviews with David Letterman, or his classic performance on Jimmy Fallon of "Raised Right Men." The studio audience can barely contain themselves.

The title of his 2011 album *Bad as Me* speaks to a question for all of us: are you as bad as me? Or am I as bad as you? The question vexed me to the point of writing a book on the subject. Spoiler alert: "Am I a good person? Well, I'm generally all right. I'm no saint . . . but I'm not Hitler."

The quote from pastor Jeff Warren strikes a chord with me and draws an uncomfortable but verified sigh: I *am* the most sinful person I know. Guess what? So are you. Yes, Warren's theologically accurate assessment is that none of us are as peachy as we think. The biblical fact is masked by hubris and delusion. Warren isn't an outlier with his statement. Any pastor worth his or her salt will say the same if they understand the concept of grace.

The brass tacks reality is this. When we look at ourselves, we grade on a curve, and it's a curve of the most biased, blinded-by-pride, I've-smoked-all-the-weed looking glass we can conceive of. Most folks play a little game called "I'm a good person." It's a clever little parlor trick where we devise a short list of ambiguous statements about doing our best, living by the golden rule, and more or less not killing anyone. Granted, the latter statement isn't ambiguous, but it's also a low bar. We like to compare our general goodness to pretty much the most egregious act a person can commit.

This is where the concept of grace enters the equation. You may find variations on the spiritual definition, but in simplistic terms, it means "undeserved favor." In other words, God provided a free and unmerited gift in the form of His Son, Jesus Christ. Through Him, we have salvation from sins and the bestowing of blessings. All of it is free to us with no way to earn this special gift. We can only say "thank you."

Maybe you're like I used to be. I had heard about Jesus dying for me plenty of times as a child and adult, but I didn't fully grasp the depth and weight of the idea. As an adult, the words "sin" and "sinner" sounded all kooky and churchy, and I didn't have any interest in the notion. First and foremost, I thought I was a pretty good dude and didn't need salvation or forgiveness. What I failed to do was take a hard look at some of my faults, like jealousy, apathy, passive-aggressiveness, lust, and general brutish behavior. The tough reality was, in a twenty-four-hour period, I spent a good sixteen hours entirely focused on *moi*. Of course, it was masked in ambition, action items, and big-ass goals. The bigger conundrum was, did I have the heavenly authority to forgive myself at a level that balances the cosmic scales?

This is where grace is an unadulterated magic, the cure to all things narcissistic. When a person accepts the grace of Jesus Christ—think of it as saying yes to free steak, lobster, and Bordeaux lunches every day for the rest of your eternal life—this strange elixir makes us gravely aware of our faults. But instead of sending us into a deep depression, grace opens our eyes to the realization that all our character deficiencies, all those mistakes, all the oopsies we shouldn't have said to our spouse, kids, coworkers, or dog, have been erased by what transpired on that cross on Golgotha. For damn sure, it. Is. *Spectacular* to comprehend.

Maybe you're thinking, "Come on. I'm not *that* bad." My bet is you're a tad disingenuous in your evaluation, and possibly cherry-picking a list that works for you. Let me phrase it the way I do in my first book. How do you compare to Mother Teresa? Or a 911 first responder? How about an ER doctor? If God measures people based on a moral meritocracy, that could get damn messy for those non-heroic types like me. Hell, yesterday at church I got sideways with a dear friend. The episode reminded me for the umpteenth time of my own depravity—a theological euphemism for being a dick. Here's a verse that summarizes the entirety of the Bible. If you don't feel the need to dissect and process the entire timeless document, try camping on this nugget from Romans 3:23–24:

> . . . for all have sinned and fall short of the glory of God, and all are justified freely by his grace through the redemption that came by Christ Jesus.

The verse is saying that we ain't all that, we screw up a lot, and we need help from an authority bigger than us. I know for certain I don't control the gateway between this life and the next, so I need some assistance for an event that is inevitable. Are there days where I'm a decent guy? Sure. But if I'm honest about my foibles, I recognize a consistent timeline of mediocrity with plenty of bad in the mix. Sure, sure, no murder or child abuse, but enough petulance to warrant a need for amazing grace.

Explore:

1) Have you thought deeply about the concept of biblical grace and what it means for you?

2) Can you imagine all your past, present, and future mistakes being truly forgiven?

WEEK 39

TO GIVE OR NOT GIVE A FUCK

*"The next time you want to withhold your help, or your
love, or your support for another for whatever the reason,
ask yourself a simple question: do the reasons you want to
withhold this reflect more on them or on you?"* [76]

—*Dan Pearce,* Single Dad Laughing

I like to play the role of judge and juror, doling out sentences of
compassion based on my subjective superiority. The act gives me a
feeling of dominance, that I'm in control of who's deserving based
on my assessment of their merit. I wish I were joking, but it's often
a good smack in the face when I catch myself withholding generosity, whether in words, action, or cash.

When I was thinking of a topic for this week's content, Veterans
Day was in the front of my mind. We hold our military men and
women in high regard, as we should. Amen. They sacrifice at the
highest level, protecting our country and others around the world.

In the midst of often irrational environments, they have to protect men, women, and children from different cultures and beliefs who may not want them in their home country. I asked a West Point friend of mine to define the role of a soldier, and the response was enlightening.

> To defend and protect the U.S. and its allies by faithfully executing the lawfully given orders of the chain of command from his/her immediate commanding officer. A soldier must do this while maintaining honor, integrity, courage, loyalty, respect, and selfless service.[77]

Following a chain of command, he or she "must do this while maintaining honor, integrity, courage, loyalty, respect, and selfless service." Sounds like a certain Jewish dude from 2,000 years ago following the will of His Father.

In this age of 24/7 grenade tossing on social media, we can point fingers at who deserves what, whether righteous or wrathful. We stand in our glass houses and cast judgement on "those other people" who don't stand for our definition of character and integrity. We do it on a very personal level when we play passive-aggressive with our spouses and friends, maybe withholding love or needed encouragement. We hold on to our money, not giving a few bucks to the guy on the corner who we proclaim most certainly made bad choices, thereby cancelling his or her worthiness of our generosity. By the way, is it *our* money? That's always an interesting theological discussion of where provision derives. On a political level, we discuss keeping people out with walls or highways, sort of like a velvet rope curbing entrance into our much cooler USA nightclub. Yes, I know, it's not fair for us to have to foot the tax bill for illegal immigrants on education, healthcare, and on and on. It's also not fair that I was born white, straight, and on soil owned by the United States. To be on the winning side of the cosmic lottery makes it damn easy to pat myself on the back and then withhold generosity.

My default on all questions is to find truth in scripture. God, show me how to discern when to give selflessly to others. The Bible has much to say about that concept, and "when" ain't got much to do with it. Let's look at an Old Testament passage about giving money.

> If anyone is poor among your fellow Israelites in any of the towns of the land the LORD your God is giving you, do not be hardhearted or tightfisted toward them. Rather, be openhanded and freely lend them whatever they need. . . . Give generously to them and do so without a grudging heart; then because of this the LORD your God will bless you in all your work and in everything you put your hand to. There will always be poor people in the land. Therefore I command you to be openhanded toward your fellow Israelites who are poor and needy in your land (Deuteronomy 15:7–8, 10–11).

It seems clear cut that the Lord gave us the United States. Sure, we traveled here, but we didn't "create" the land and resources. There will always be poor people, and we're commanded to give freely with no gritting of teeth. I've heard arguments that this is specific to the Israelites of that time, thereby giving us an out, or skewing it a bit to say this refers to our countrymen, like 'Mercans only. But this position creates some messy theology when looking at the entirety of scripture, particularly when we look at the life of Jesus. I heard one of the most respected theologians in the country, Tim Keller, preach on this a few years ago in Dallas. He pulled no punches in saying we Dallasites, and anyone claiming to be a Christ follower, need this same attitude of giving generously of what's not yours in the first place.

In relation to helping others who may not look, speak or share our U.S. birthright, the parable of the good Samaritan sets the high watermark for neighbors never being strangers. (I didn't include verse 25, where it's clear the person asking the question is a Jewish expert in the law.)

> But he wanted to justify himself, so he asked Jesus, "And who is my neighbor?"
>
> In reply Jesus said: "A man was going down from Jerusalem to Jericho, when he was attacked by robbers. They stripped him of his clothes, beat him and went away, leaving him half dead. A priest happened to be going down the same road, and when he saw the man, he passed by on the other side. So too, a Levite, when he came to the place and saw him, passed by on the other side. But a Samaritan, as he traveled, came where the man was; and when he saw him, he took pity on him. He went to him and bandaged his wounds, pouring on oil and wine. Then he put the man on his own donkey, brought him to an inn and took care of him. The next day he took out two denarii and gave them to the innkeeper. 'Look after him,' he said, 'and when I return, I will reimburse you for any extra expense you may have.'

"Which of these three do you think was a neighbor to the man who fell into the hands of robbers?"

The expert in the law replied, "The one who had mercy on him."

Jesus told him, "Go and do likewise" (Luke 10:29–37).

Jews and Samaritans despised each other and were mortal enemies. Remember, this is pre-civil rights, pre-medieval times—like *way* back in the day. In the modern era, the equivalent would be a story of a Black fella stopping to help an injured KKK member . . . in the heart of the Mississippi Delta . . . in 1930.

Like our military servicemen, Christ served for the greater good at an an unfathomable level when we add the full weight of all sins for all of mankind for all of history. The entirety of Christ's life is about giving. I couldn't find any scriptures where Jesus withheld generosity. No, scripture is filled with one example after another of extreme, breathtaking love. In the Gospel of John, He lays down a statement that stops us in our tracks.

Greater love has no one than this: to lay down one's life for one's friends (John 15:13).

He ultimately gave his life for all of mankind throughout history. All He asks of us is to give generously with time, talents, and money and to treat everyone like we've never met a stranger. For damn sure we got the eazy-peezy part of the deal.

Explore:

1) Christian theology states that Jesus Christ laid down His life to erase your mistakes. Can a person be indifferent to such an astonishing claim?

2) Are you generous with your time and money? How about with people who may have made poor choices and ended up in a bad spot?

WEEK 40

ARE YOU SUCCESSFUL?

"It had long since come to my attention that people of accomplishment rarely sat back and let things happen to them. They went out and happened to things."

—*attributed to Leonardo da Vinci*

Success is a bear to navigate. It's safe to say our culture is consumed with the idea. There are a multitude of definitions for each of us. It could mean a title, a neighborhood, or, of course, the number of zeros in the bank account. In the last decade, new measures have arisen in the form of followers, "Likes," Klout scores, and whether you're an influencer.

A friend sent a daily devotional to me one morning from Christine Caine. I'd never heard of her. Turns out she's an Aussie who, with her husband, founded the A21 Campaign, which seeks to abolish human trafficking. Damn, that's cool. I love hearing about Jesus freaks on the other side of the planet, working under His umbrella to impact lives. Makes me get on my apologetics horse and wonder why they aren't doing this under the mighty name of spiritualism or atheism. Yes, I know there are non-faith-based NGOs out there, but lots of 'em sure lead with that mighty cross. But I digress. Caine's devotional about success had this description from God's Word:

Success

a) ~~is having money or power~~
b) ~~is avoiding criticism~~
c) ~~is having prestige, position, or prominence~~
d) **is discovering and doing the will of God for your life.**[78]

It's a loaded group of bullet points, and the concluding statement is also a head-scratcher. I'm not saying she needs to clarify, but it *is* the question of the ages: "What is God's plan for my life!?" We often throw up our hands in exasperation as we navigate the minefields of life. My church has an excellent program called Repurposed that helps people discern their God-given gifts. Do the answers come overnight? Not necessarily. Only a small percentage of people know as precocious eighteen-year-olds whether athletics, coding, or music naturally emanates from their pores. Most of us have to stab wildly in fits and starts, hoping we evolve into a passionate purpose for waking up each day. Often, we do have clarity of our strengths and core competencies, but self-doubt and sabotage claw away at our confidence. The *Harvard Business Review* article "Why Talented People Don't Use Their Strengths" is a good read on the subject. It essentially says to keep it simple and focus on what comes easily for you. Pay attention to things that your mind naturally drifts toward. Are you able to quickly develop marketing ideas? Consider it a gift. Can you effortlessly crunch through a P&L statement or balance sheet and see budget issues in the numbers? Follow that trail, young man, and go west. Do you find yourself inquisitive about social issues? A nonprofit might be an avenue to explore.

Here's the tension. The *HBR* article is solid and applicable to Caine's bullet points. But in the upside-down kingdom of heaven, the Lord may have different outcomes in mind. In other words, how often do you turn on the daily news in any medium and come away encouraged to forget about money, power, prestige, and prominence? Sure, maybe on the Hallmark Channel, but I can't recall too many performance reviews or investor updates where they led with this verse from James 2:5:

> Listen, my dear brothers and sisters: Has not God chosen those who are poor in the eyes of the world to be rich in faith and to inherit the kingdom he promised those who love him?

There are key words in scripture worth noting, such as "therefore" when Paul is laying down some heavy theology, or when Christ speaks to crowds, or when God the Father says in Mark 9:7 and Luke 9:35, "This is my Son, whom I love. Listen to him!" In this case, James, the brother of Jesus, is saying that the poor among us have won the real lottery because they have a deeper faith than those with wealth. As much as we may not like that theological fact, we've experienced it. It's the rare bird who has genuine humility and a bright yellow Corvette. Yet how many folks do we know who've been pummeled from a sickness or massive failure and carry a deep reservoir of sumpin-sumpin—a special patience and ability to answer the phone at 2 a.m. or a masterful ability to listen and pray for your wounds without firing off a quick fix? The James passage is not an obscure cherry I picked. In some of the most challenging and inspired verses of all scripture, we find these anti-world nuggets in the Sermon on the Mount from Matthew 5:3–12:

> Blessed are the poor in spirit,
>> for theirs is the kingdom of heaven.
> Blessed are those who mourn,
>> for they will be comforted.
> Blessed are the meek,
>> for they will inherit the earth.
> Blessed are those who hunger and thirst for righteousness,
>> for they will be filled.
> Blessed are the merciful,
>> for they will be shown mercy.
> Blessed are the pure in heart,
>> for they will see God.
> Blessed are the peacemakers,
>> for they will be called children of God.
> Blessed are those who are persecuted because of righteousness,
>> for theirs is the kingdom of heaven.
> Blessed are you when people insult you, persecute you and falsely say all kinds of evil against you because of me. Rejoice and be glad, because great is your reward in heaven, for in the same way they persecuted the prophets who were before you.

Again, the world does not amplify this message. Not at all; it says the opposite. Get yours because YOLO and FOMO, and the clock is ticking. Christ's message in these verses is a life we're incapable of manufacturing on our own. Only with His grace, plus our wild abandonment of worldly goals to follow Him, do we have a chance of grasping these holy mysteries.

The journey to live out the Beatitudes may mirror what da Vinci is often quoted as saying. Because he lived during the early Renaissance, I'll assume his thoughts were of a deeper place about righteous purpose and mercy as spelled out by our Lord, and not a prophecy of my LinkedIn profile. I'm hopeful we can pursue a different definition of success that brings clap emojis from heaven.

Explore:

1) Would you say you are rich in faith in the same way as someone who is poor by worldly standards?
2) Are the Beatitudes easy for you to grasp, or do they appear out of sorts in comparison to Western culture?

WEEK 41

I SHOULD BE ARRESTED

"If you knew the full condition of my heart, my fantasies and grievances, my anxieties and my darkest solitary thoughts, you would declare me a danger to myself and others. I cannot be entrusted with power by myself, certainly not with celebrity, and neither can you." [79]

—*Andy Crouch*

I like to argue with Jesus. Part of every day is spent with my two personalities—might as well call them my inner "childrens"—*Justification* and *Rationalization*. They're close cousins of *Snark* and *Bark*, the two I prefer when I'm full of piss and vinegar. During the moments, hours, or days when this foulness arises, I run down my list of good deeds to offset the negative. I then consider what Christ considers bad behavior in the verses below and begin my assault with J & R leading the charge. "I said a prayer for that guy . . . that should negate the middle finger to the Range Rover . . . I gave so-and-so a

ride to church. Cool, the scales of justice are for moi. Let's disregard
my glee in hearing about my buddy's struggling business."

> For out of the heart come evil thoughts—murder,
> adultery, sexual immorality, theft, false testimony,
> slander (Matthew 15:19).

The quote from pastor Andy Crouch above catches my attention
for two reasons: 1) It sounds like something from a stand-up comedian (insert laugh track). And 2) His truth is all our truth, and
if we deny it, we're lying. When I think about the mesmerizing
power of fame, I often laugh when critics say the Rolling Stones
should hang it up. Yeah, sure, how crazy to want 70,000 people to
pay $100 a night for a chance to scream in adoration. Who wants
beautiful women around the world clamoring for your bed, wrin-
kles be damned? Plus, the best food and wine are all yours, and
for "Keef," all the best pharmaceutical extracurriculars. Nope, not
interested . . . said no one ever.

But the other end of the glamour is the dark stuff—the pho-
bias, the anxieties, the "grievances." What a perfect word choice
by Crouch. His honesty is pitch-perfect. We can't trust ourselves.
That's the scary part of our magnificent minds. They're capable
of spellbinding value for humanity, and they're equally capable of
deep darkness. What captures my attention, and is a primary thesis
in my book *I'm Not Hitler,* is when we trick ourselves by elevating
our merit. In other words, has there ever been a day—hell, how
about eight hours—where I was fantasy- or grievance-free? No
chance. John Eldredge puts it this way:

> Most of the misery we suffer on this planet is the
> fruit of the human heart gone bad. . . . Any honest

person knows this. We know we are not what we
were meant to be. . . . Most of the world religions
concur on this point. Something needs to be done.
Jews try to keep the Law. Buddhists follow the
Eightfold Path. Muslims live by the Five Pillars.
Many Christians try church attendance and moral
living. You'd think, with all the effort, humanity
would be on top of things by now.[80]

For clarity, a friend of mine pushed back on me in response to a
recent blog post, and he's right. As a Christ follower, I am a new
creation. All my mistakes, past and present, have been erased, per
these verses and plenty of others.

> Grace and peace to you from God our Father and
> the Lord Jesus Christ, who gave himself for our
> sins to rescue us from the present evil age, accord-
> ing to the will of our God and Father, to whom be
> glory for ever and ever. Amen (Galatians 1:3–5).

> In him we have redemption through his blood, the
> forgiveness of sins, in accordance with the riches
> of God's grace that he lavished on us (Ephesians
> 1:7–8).

What my buddy is saying in relation to these verses is that I no longer have to despair over the thoughts I share with Crouch. From
Christ's point of view, all the darkness in my mind and outward
fumbles have been absorbed by Him. Yes, the remnants still exist.
In other words, the cancer will not be fully eradicated until the
next life, the real one in the big show of eternity.

Here's some fantastic theology for us to own. The beauty of Christ is that He has forgiven me for the thirty to fifty shit thoughts I have per day. He also provides absolute truth and infinite love in a single being. What does that mean for us? My Wednesday group of Jesus freak dudes once discussed the importance of checks and balances. We serve as a band of brothers who encourage, listen to, and challenge each other to find and hold on to the singular and universal truth of Christ. In Christianese, it's called "community." We need close friends and mentors to keep us on the narrow path, and yes, it is narrow, as Christ says.

> Enter through the narrow gate. For wide is the gate and broad is the road that leads to destruction, and many enter through it. But small is the gate and narrow the road that leads to life, and only a few find it (Matthew 7:13–14).

Ask ten people for their version of truth, and you'll quickly see how modern culture loves it some pluralism: "You live your truth, I'll live mine." It sounds chummy, but it has glaring holes you can drive a '75 Eldorado through. Ask ten more people to share some of their inner darkness. You'll see how Crouch's honesty is yours, theirs, and mine too.

Explore:

1) If you're honest, are your thoughts pure and blemish-free, or are they similar to Andy Crouch's?
2) Do you fully comprehend and own what Jesus has done for you and all of mankind as explained in the Galatians and Ephesians verses? In other words, do you understand that you've been rescued from yourself?

WEEK 42

OUR NEIGHBOR THE SAINT

*" 'If we can somehow rid ourselves of illusions,' he said. 'The
illusion that we are greater or lesser than we are. The illusion
that we're going to save the world. There are a lot of illusions
that people walk around with. I would love to be able to be
present in every moment I have.' "* [81]

—*Fred Rogers*

The *Merriam-Webster* definition of *saint* says, "one officially recognized especially through canonization as preeminent for holi-
ness."[82] I bet Mr. Rogers would've said, "A saint is someone who is
always nice to people, someone you can trust will give him or her-
self for others." Fred Rogers created a magical world of education
for children while also living out the purest definition of sainthood.
Millions of kids learned about the world in an innocent way before
stepping out into the actual arena, where dragons roam in the form
of adults. His lessons stuck, as did his gentle effervescence.

The 1998 *Esquire* article "Can You Say . . . Hero?" by Tom
Junod is a good starting place for reading about how Rogers

impacted lives. The new film *A Beautiful Day in the Neighborhood*, with Tom Hanks portraying the iconic figure, is now available to watch. The reviews were universally strong, but some have said that even Hanks at his best can't quite capture the essence of the man who had a fortitude of love that few may ever match. The film is based on the relationship that evolved between Rogers and journalist Lloyd Vogel. It shows the universal appeal of someone who exudes 24/7 grace and how a person who bleeds it with such an open spigot will connect across racial divides. As Junod writes in the *Esquire* piece,

> He finds me, because that's what Mister Rogers *does*—he looks, and then he finds. I'm standing against a wall, listening to a bunch of mooks from Long Island discuss the strange word—*charis*—he has written down on each of the autographs he gave them. First mook: "He says it's the Greek word for grace." Second mook: "Huh. That's cool. I'm glad I know that. Now, what the fuck is grace?" First mook: "Looks like you're gonna have to break down and buy a dictionary." Second mook: "Fuck that. What I'm buying is a ticket to the fucking *Lotto*. I just met Mister Rogers—this is *definitely* my lucky day."[83]

Hey, if a few f-bombs need to be dropped to open the door for the Lord's grace, by all means, drop 'em. Rogers attended Pittsburgh Theological Seminary and was ordained as a Presbyterian minister in 1963. He was a devout Christ follower who started every day with scripture reading and prayer. It's safe to assume he knew how powerful grace can be in a person's life.

Here's the thing, though: while Rogers knew his purpose was to spark the imaginations of children with puppets and trolleys, wowza, did he leave a Sasquatch-sized footprint on setting an example for the equality for all people. I didn't put two and two together till I reread the Luke 10 scripture about the good Samaritan. I then realized how cagey a bird Rogers was as he sang "Please, won't you be my neighbor." Astonishing—and I may be the last guy at the party to realize the connection.

But he wanted to justify himself, so he asked Jesus, "And who is my neighbor?"

In reply Jesus said: "A man was going down from Jerusalem to Jericho, when he was attacked by robbers. They stripped him of his clothes, beat him and went away, leaving him half dead. A priest happened to be going down the same road, and when he saw the man, he passed by on the other side. So too, a Levite, when he came to the place and saw him, passed by on the other side. But a Samaritan, as he traveled, came where the man was; and when he saw him, he took pity on him. He went to him and bandaged his wounds, pouring on oil and wine. Then he put the man on his own donkey, brought him to an inn and took care of him. The next day he took out two denarii and gave them to the innkeeper. 'Look after him,' he said, 'and when I return, I will reimburse you for any extra expense you may have.'

"Which of these three do you think was a neighbor to the man who fell into the hands of robbers?"

The expert in the law replied, "The one who had mercy on him."

Jesus told him, "Go and do likewise" (Luke 10:29–37).

This was Mr. Rogers's way of teaching children at a young age that racism is for jackass morons (but he had too much integrity and gentleness to expose children to such crude grown-up words). Yet what a reminder; he sang the request 912 times over thirty years. How brilliant considering the simple melody and our tendency to internalize songs.

In another grace-filled remembrance of Rogers, the Vanity Fair interview "Mister Rogers's Gay, Black Friend François Clemmons Wears Tiaras Now" with the actor-singer who played Officer Clemmons on the program for thirty years speaks volumes about Rogers's deep layers. They developed a close friendship, and Rogers knew his closeted friend was gay. Clemmons says he never felt judged, even though Rogers had to draw a line in the sand for how much viewers of the racially charged late sixties and early seventies could stomach. Rogers was smart enough to know that TV audiences were challenged enough by seeing a Black man interacting with a white man at that time, let alone a Black man who was also gay. How many 2020 employers would take that position? Sure, it's easy to say "I would" with *Modern Family* and *Will & Grace*, among numerous others, on the air. Keep in mind that ABC cancelled Ellen's late-nineties sitcom after she announced she was gay. Fred Rogers kept his friend and coworker employed on the show regardless of his sexuality and took sledgehammer swings at showing acceptance. The website Great Big Story has a wonderful video called "The Officer of Make Believe: Being Black in 'Mister Rogers' Neighborhood' " where Clemmons discusses how Rogers knew exactly what he was doing in pushing the boundaries of acceptance. At 1:25 of the clip, Rogers washes Officer Clemmons's feet. Hmm . . . I remember a certain guy in scripture who did the same thing.

> Jesus knew that the Father had put all things under his power, and that he had come from God and was returning to God; so he got up from the meal, took off his outer clothing, and wrapped a towel around his waist. After that, he poured water into a basin and began to wash his disciples' feet, drying them with the towel that was wrapped around him (John 13:3–5).

How endearing to see the legacy of a man steeped in gentleness and love continue to resonate years after his death. A man who starred in a cheesy-looking little public television show, who did not crown himself as more important than anyone else. How many lessons of selflessness and true masculinity can I learn from a man who wanted everyone to be his neighbor?

Explore:

1) Is Mr. Rogers a better definition of manhood than John Wayne? Should toughness be measured by love?

2) Do you find it astonishing that Christ would lower Himself to wash the feet of people? What does this gesture say about His expectations for us?

WEEK 43

THE PRISON OF
THANKLESSNESS

*"Even the worst that has ever happened to
you could have been worse."* [84]

—*Mokokoma Mokhonoana*

I don't mean to brag, but I am a fifth-degree black belt in the art of bitching. Each day, I put on my best Miss America pageant smile and feign contentment as I wave to the crowds. Yet my inside voice tells another story—a thirty-chapter manifesto, a cauldron boiling with frustration. What's the main ingredient? Yessir, a heaping helping of entitlement.

It shocks me to consider this fundamental flaw in my character. Actually, come to think of it, I shouldn't be shocked. It seems the human condition is to 1) want, 2) crave, and 3) strive to obtain. When the desired outcome is not achieved, the prison of thanklessness creeps in and takes up an entrenched position in my mind. I don't think I'm alone in this struggle. The collective "we" are bombarded with thousands of sales pitches each day in our consumerist culture. My car, clothes, glasses, socks, soap, and toothpaste all claim to be the god of true happiness after one more purchase. According to Finder.com, Americans were projected to spend $87 billion on Black Friday and Cyber Monday in 2019 to get our shopping fix.[85] While Giving Tuesday is a newer "holiday" and has gotten more and more popular each year, it lags behind by a country mile ($380 million given in 2018, according to Nonprofits Source[86]). The insatiable shopper in me says the two days will never close the delta, which speaks to our inherent nature.

That is the deep wound, the desire for more, and the sense of entitlement driving it. We compare and sulk, or compare and go harder to catch up. The momentary feeling of "I've arrived" is quickly jettisoned when I see others with a bigger, shinier position in life and the accoutrements that come with it. Where it gets damn nasty is when it affects my worldview. When I'm in comparison-entitlement mode, I'm on edge, which, for my wiring, makes me prone to argue instead of empathize, to lash out instead of listen.

The only effective solution I've found is a posture of gratitude, but jeepers, is it tough to bend to that position when wealth appears to be all around. I heard an interview with actor Henry Winkler (if you're of a certain age, you'll recall that he was one of the most famous people on the planet in the mid-seventies) where he said, "I live by two words—gratitude and tenacity. Tenacity gets me where I want to go and gratitude doesn't allow me to be angry along the way."[87] Amen to you, Arthur Herbert Fonzarelli. Amen.

Scripture enforces the need for mercy and grace in my life and gently (or sometimes forcibly) reminds me of what I truly deserve. In three crisp but explosive verses, Ephesians 2:3–5 says it all.

> All of us also lived among them at one time, grati-
> fying the cravings of our flesh and following its
> desires and thoughts. Like the rest, we were by
> nature deserving of wrath. But because of his great
> love for us, God, who is rich in mercy, made us
> alive with Christ even when we were dead in trans-
> gressions—it is by grace you have been saved.

Yes, that's much bigger than a shopping jones. That's some grade-A theology making the point "I deserve nothing." Not happiness, not the big career, not love, not the air I breathe. Please hear me: I'm not recommending that we all buy shirts that say, "Hi, I'm a dirtbag." I am saying that I have to get over myself and question this idea of what's rightfully mine. This includes the realization that without the mercy and grace of Christ, my destination is a very bad place. Yes, I know the idea of hell is not popular. The real truth is we're okay with it as long as it's an eternal hotel for someone else. The heavier theology, which I've stated in the past, is that God doesn't send us there; we choose it. We are some rebellious "sumbitches," and we very much want our way, just like we want our stuff on Black Friday. Our loving and gracious God has given us free will to choose whether we want to know Him, trust Him, and, yes, surrender to Him as the greater loving authority or whether we want to do life on our own. When we choose the latter by our own volition, He, with pained graciousness, allows us the permanent and eternal choice.

Yep, I hear ya. You can buck and bitch. I didn't like the concept either until I came to know God through Christ when I was thirty-two years old. After twenty years, I still wrestle with entitlement, but now I wash it with an infinite waterfall of mercy and grace. It's taken me years to fully comprehend verses like this little gem in 1 John 4:19: "We love because he first loved us." That verse comes after verse 7, which says, "for love comes from God." That's can sound all hippy-dippy, but it's saying all the empathy, patience, laughter, and humility—the opposite feelings of bitterness and any perceived lacking—that good stuff came from Him because He created us and loved us before we even considered His relevance. When I recognize this cosmic fact, everything changes. If I start my day with "Thank you, Lord, for friends. Thank you for walking and talking. Thank you for thinking and laughing. Thank you for saving me from myself," entitlement gets kicked to the curb—the same as I should've been, but for His mercy.

Explore:

1) Do you find yourself on edge due to frustration with status? Is the feeling due to entitlement?

2) Does our culture say we deserve it all: happiness, comfort, provision? Is this true?

WEEK 44

PLEASE MAKE ME FAMOUS!

"I have always been famous—you just didn't know it yet!" [88]

—Lady Gaga

The 2017 *Forbes* article "One in Four Millennials Would Quit Their Job to Be Famous" exposes darkness in those young whippersnappers. How bizarre to only care about empty fame as a goal in life. Ah, if only I could look down my nose at that demographic and not evaluate my own desires with similar disdain. Wouldn't it be nice if I had the same inner glee with four "Likes" compared to 100? Or think of how we frame an autograph of a beloved sports hero or celebrity. Maybe we like to brush up against greatness as a way to prop up our lack of perceived luster.

I recently rewatched Ron Howard's 2016 documentary *The Beatles: Eight Days a Week*. This time, the spectacle of Beatlemania stirred new thoughts on the idea of fame. I can't think of another cultural event that rivals this as ground zero for celebrity worship. In the fifty years since the Liverpool lads exploded onto the global scene, our devotion to stardom has yet to wane. Now the newest option—social media influencer—has expanded the fold. I like to get lost in nerdy YouTube videos about production techniques and how iconic guitar and drum sounds were created. This leads down rabbit holes featuring video gems like ten-year-old Yoyoka playing Led Zeppelin. When I hop over to check out some Instagram feeds, I cringe. Talented and attractive? Yes. Yet all of the posts on some users' pages are of no one other than dear old self, and the majority have a come-hither vibe. No group pics with friends, no beautiful sunsets, not even a food shot. Thousands of fitness men and women on social media do their own versions of seminude selfies to gain attention.

No doubt the Beatles' talent was groundbreaking. Volumes have been written on the multitude of ways they influenced melody, lyrics, production, and concerts as landmark events. The thing that stood out to me on this viewing of the documentary was actress Sigourney Weaver discussing how she had to be perfectly dolled up when attending the show. She *knew* John would fall in love with her among the mass of fans. She laughs now, but doesn't her desire speak to a deeper place in all of us? The craving to be known, to be loved, to be recognized. Yes, they're all healthy aspirations up to a point, but there's also a festering emptiness that shows our dissatisfaction with life and self.

The Beatles' story peers into human depravity in two events in their history (which, unlike a non-famous person, becomes our history). Many of us can recall exactly where we were upon hearing the news of John Lennon's 1980 murder by unemployed security guard Mark Chapman, who later said he was incensed by Lennon's lifestyle. His dissatisfaction and mental illness moved him to horrific action, as did a less publicized stabbing of George Harrison in his home in 1999. A *New York Times article* said "evidence emerged that the assailant may have harbored a dangerous obsession with the band."[89]

It's easy to dismiss those individuals as extreme examples. But we tell on ourselves when we check our "Like" status, as mentioned above. My personal enchantment with fame is a delicate balance between competency and empty narcissism. Yes, I want to be good at any endeavor or project I attack. All of us should have a robust desire to max out our aptitudes and talent with elbow grease and grit. The *Forbes* article speaks to the current zeitgeist— a different measure not based on merit, giving rationale to the hunger.

> In a time when we've elected a man who has "fired" Gene Simmons and Dennis Rodman on national television to the highest office in the land, complete with all its trappings of immense global power, why the heck wouldn't millennials prioritize notoriety?[90]

When I turn to scripture, I'm reminded of how our yearning for fame is a symptom of our rooted need for healing. Every individual on the planet struggles with a measure of brokenness; some with obvious physical ailments, others with cracked psyches. In Luke 6:17–19, there are groups of people as hopeful as the Beatles' fans.

> He went down with them and stood on a level place. A large crowd of his disciples was there and a great number of people from all over Judea, from Jerusalem, and from the coastal region around Tyre and Sidon, who had come to hear him and to be healed of their diseases. Those troubled by

impure spirits were cured, and the people all tried
to touch him, because power was coming from
him and healing them all.

"He went down with them and stood on a level place." Reminiscent
of a stage, where large crowds congregate in united hope to hear
powered sounds that might heal something inside. Not only millennials, but all of us for two millennia have been looking for
someone to restore us with the sound and power of his or her
words. While I am a rabid fan of the Beatles, I hope my adoring
worship is reserved for the one Israelite who satisfies my misguided hopes that fame can never fulfill.

Explore:

1) Do you find yourself wishing you were famous? Why
   would that bring you additional happiness?

2) Is there a festering wound in your psyche you wish could
   be healed?

WEEK 45

I NEED AN ETERNAL NAP

*"Every person needs to take one day away. A day in which
one consciously separates the past from the future. Jobs, lovers,
family, employers, and friends can exist one day without any
one of us, and if our egos permit us to confess, they could exist
eternally in our absence."* [91]

—*Maya Angelou*

Last Friday at 5:00 while driving home in my Jeep, I caught myself
saying, "Get the fuck outta my way you slow muthuh-fuckuhs."
Not my inside voice. Out. Loud. In other words, "all you peeps
need to get out of my way so I can get shit done." How many
ways am I whackadoo in that brief snapshot of my Friday? For
those who say, "I would never say or think that," you's some lying
muthuh-fuckuhs.

This followed on the heels of a discussion with my Friday men's
group about the idea of resting. As in, how often do we actually
take time to halt the busyness of life? The back-and-forth centered
on the biblical concept of Sunday being a day of decompressing,

replenishing, and thanking the Lord. We are to follow what God did on the seventh day—not that I think He's in need of naptime like us. He was setting a precedent for us to follow in Genesis 2:2–3.

> By the seventh day God had finished the work he had been doing; so on the seventh day he rested from all his work. Then God blessed the seventh day and made it holy, because on it he rested from all the work of creating that he had done.

The dialogue that Friday morning was rich. A couple of us said that our go-go-go culture and insistence on pushing past the need for rest and sleep is a symptom of not trusting where we are in life; therefore, we have no time to turn off the motor. The clock is ticking, I'm running the show—not God—and I've decided I'm behind in the game for that day, week, or decade. Isn't this the deeper issue? A toxic, frenetic pace to arrive at some destination we've convinced ourselves will provide complete happiness? It seems to be a race to accumulate a significant savings account for retirement and then enjoy the good life. This concept brings pause, particularly in light of a recent lunch where I heard a no-nonsense, focus-on-the-right-things pastor say, "Good luck finding scriptures on retirement." Confused, nervous laughter followed from the audience.

So then what are we racing and resting toward? Is retirement the goal? It depends on who's running your life. If you buy into the idea of "work hard so you can play hard to cash out and count seashells on the beach with piña colada in hand," then giddyup and push hard to achieve a comfortable life.

Or we can look to scripture as the proper lighthouse for telling us which direction to sail. If we decide to make God and His word our final authority, a new finish line consumes our vision. From 2 Timothy 4:7–8:

> I have fought the good fight, I have finished the race, I have kept the faith. Now there is in store for me the crown of righteousness, which the Lord, the righteous Judge, will award to me on that day—and not only to me, but also to all who have longed for his appearing.

If there's a question as to what race Paul is referring to, we jump up a couple of verses to the beginning of the chapter, where he says in verses 1–2:

> In the presence of God and of Christ Jesus, who will judge the living and the dead, and in view of his appearing and his kingdom, I give you this charge: Preach the word; be prepared in season and out of season; correct, rebuke and encourage—with great patience and careful instruction.

"I give you this charge." Scripture is fascinating when we realize how the verses are directed toward us. Paul and Timothy were not super Christians donning tights and capes. They were normal schmoes like you and I, which means God is telling us the same message He told them. Our focus is to be all about the gospel.

Let me be clear. There are seasons of life where work must end and a transition is needed. That time will differ per person based on their wiring and chosen field. The primary point is, yes, we should ease up and rest in trusting the Lord's chess moves in our lives. At the same time, don't look at this life as the one that counts the most. The logic seems irrefutable: if heaven is real and eternal, and if this life is, at best, eighty to ninety years tops, then we should follow Paul's charge to Timothy and see our work on this side of heaven as an environment to affect others in the name of Christ. For me, I'll look for opportunities to "preach" or explain the value of scripture and try to turn my gaze outward to sacrifice for friends and strangers. It'll be messy, and my selfish navel will fight for gazing, but my goal will be to rest in the Lord. As David said in Psalm 62:5–6,

> Yes, my soul, find rest in God;
> my hope comes from him.
> Truly he is my rock and my salvation.

Explore:

1) Is it challenging for you to turn off work, the phone, and the computer and simply rest?

2) If life is a race, do you know which finish line you're charging toward? How will you define a win?

WEEK 46

MY AMBITION TO STRIVE

"At the age of six I wanted to be a cook. At seven I wanted to be Napoleon. And my ambition has been growing steadily ever since." [92]

—*Salvador Dalí*

Nothing stirs my inner moxie machine like some good ol' New York City-focused drama. Apple TV's new offering *The Morning Show* is the perfect prescription to get us all jazzed up to conquer the world. It features great actors reciting crisp dialogue as they portray how to navigate the crushing pace of a national morning news show. Think *Good Morning America* and the eruption after Matt Lauer was fired for allegations of sexual misconduct. The show pulls no punches with stellar performances by all, including Reese Witherspoon, Billy Crudup, Steve Carell, and Jennifer Aniston. This is a high watermark of writing and acting and shows how messy our lives are behind the veneer of TV and social media.

What makes *The Morning Show* compelling is the multifaceted personal points of view of the characters. Steve Carell, in particular, captures a fascinating portrayal of someone who may have crossed a line, maybe? Or were the participants naive, complicit, or calculating a career move with sex as the currency? The question of "Were his actions egregious?" must be evaluated, and woo-doggie, is it messy and thought-provoking to watch.

Of the many layers of broadcast fame, corporate politics, sexism, and personal loyalty, there's an underlying question of that wonderful attribute, *ambition*. Or is it a vice? Hmmm. Our culture seems to place ambition high on a pedestal as a positive, driving force. When focused in the right direction, yes. However, often our superpowers end up being used for evil instead of good. Personally, it takes maybe half a second for my ambition to laser-focus on creating *my* goals, what's best for *my* life, and how I can best achieve *my* plans . . . oh, and maybe God approves. In fact, He for damn sure better be helping MY plans! Doesn't He know His damn role in MY world!?

It's a fine line we walk. Yes, use your God-given gifts. Yes, work hard to provide a good product and service for your customers. Yes, play nice and help your coworkers and the company that pays you. However, don't let ambition become an ego on steroids. In fact, the word "ambition" is used eight times in the Bible, and only twice is it positive.

> It has always been my **ambition** to preach the gospel where Christ was not known, so that I would not be building on someone else's foundation (Romans 15:20).

> Yet we urge you, brothers and sisters, to do so more and more, and to make it your **ambition** to

lead a quiet life: You should mind your own business and work with your hands, just as we told you (1 Thessalonians 4:10–11).

For I am afraid that when I come I may not find you as I want you to be, and you may not find me as you want me to be. I fear that there may be discord, jealousy, fits of rage, selfish **ambition**, slander, gossip, arrogance and disorder (2 Corinthians 12:20).

The acts of the flesh are obvious: sexual immorality, impurity and debauchery; idolatry and witchcraft; hatred, discord, jealousy, fits of rage, selfish **ambition**, dissensions, factions . . . (Galatians 5:19–20).

The former preach Christ out of selfish **ambition**, not sincerely, supposing that they can stir up trouble for me while I am in chains (Philippians 1:17).

Do nothing out of selfish **ambition** or vain conceit. Rather, in humility value others above yourselves (Philippians 2:3).

But if you harbor bitter envy and selfish **ambition** in your hearts, do not boast about it or deny the truth (James 3:14).

For where you have envy and selfish **ambition**, there you find disorder and every evil practice (James 3:16).

Easy, cowboy. Before you point out that scripture says "selfish ambition," keep in mind that the entirety of the Bible paints an image of people as the Mount Rushmore of narcissism. In other words, our nature is to look out for number one before looking outward to others. Think I'm off? Try this. Ask yourself and your friends whether they want a life of service or comfort. In other words, when not working, do you (or they) want entertainment, vacations, more money, more clothes, bigger houses, more wine, and more food? Or do you want to volunteer, serve others, and give your stuff away? How are the scales weighing out? Black Friday and Giving Tuesday seem to answer the question of where our hearts are regarding consumerism and altruism, and ambition fuels the hunger. Here's a clarifying verse regarding my ability to steer ambition. It puts me on my heels every time, particularly since I like to say, "I go with my gut."

> The heart is deceitful above all things, and desperately sick; who can understand it? (Jeremiah 17:9 ESV).

Stunning how a book that's 3,400 years old, give or take, can speak to every facet of our lives. Jealousy, fits of rage, dissension, gossip, arrogance, sexual immorality, bitter envy, and vain conceit? Naw, all that ancient literature ain't relevant in our picturesque times (he says, dripping with sarcasm). Therefore, I better keep tight reins on my ambition. I better douse it with a big bucket of heavenly grace before I let it run rampant. For me, that means daily surrender to the tune of, "Lord, this day is Yours. You allowed me to wake up; use me as You see fit, not as I think best. Make my efforts focused on others and not on myself."

In "Christianese," you often hear the phrase "It's a heart issue," meaning "am I acting in a way that's ultimately glorifying

God or moi?" Even the idea of "glorifying God" is an ambiguous endeavor on plenty of days. What does glorifying look like—with ambition in the mix—when the boss is pushing hard for Q4 sales quotas to meet the earnings forecast? That's the brass tacks. Maybe it means we give credit to others when we were responsible for more value. Maybe we allow a coworker to move ahead on the vaunted career ladder, and we take a backseat so they can accelerate. Yikes—that doesn't sit well in our me-me-go-go culture. As always, we have to decide whether we're running the show and our lives or whether's there a higher authority who governs how we strive, and for what outcome.

Lord, eliminate *my* ambition. Make any ambition a lifelong endeavor of plans and goals that help others shine. Help me strive to make Your grace known. If I lose in the process, teach me to smile when You win.

Explore:

1) Is your ambition fueled by self-focus, or are you pushing hard so others can win? Be honest. Your personal career achievements should be a sacrificial win for your team, not only you.

2) Are you striving for more stuff, or are you creating bandwidth for more service?

WEEK 47

BLESSINGS AND BATTLES EVERY YEAR

"I hope that in this year to come, you make mistakes. Because if you are making mistakes, then you are making new things, trying new things, learning, living, pushing yourself, changing yourself, changing your world. You're doing things you've never done before, and more importantly, you're doing something. So that's my wish for you, and all of us, and my wish for myself. Make new mistakes. Make glorious, amazing mistakes. Make mistakes nobody's ever made before. Don't freeze, don't stop, don't worry that it isn't good enough, or it isn't perfect, whatever it is: art, or love, or work or family or life. Whatever it is you're scared of doing, do it. Make your mistakes, next year and forever." [93]

—Neil Gaiman

Tick-tock-tick-tock. Not only has another year passed, but a decade too. I'm convinced that twenty-four hours are not what they used to be. For damn sure what looks like twenty-four hours passing is really only fourteen, maybe fifteen at the most. Hence the reason it seems each year races past at an accelerated pace.

As the 2019 holidays came to a close, I felt low-level anxiety. "Uh oh. Here comes another year of battle. What are my goals? Where can I make the most impact with things of eternal significance? I don't think I want to get out of bed for 2020." The last sentence was the genuine reveal. There was a sense of dread, of not wanting to lean into the struggle anymore. You feel me? Life is a fight, no doubt—ntrying to generate the moxie and the sumpin-sumpin to not quit. Thankfully, I came across that Neil Gaiman quote. There are similar memes all over the internet, but sometimes the real stuff rises to the top. It's the line about "Don't freeze, don't stop, don't worry that it isn't good enough," and of course the mention of being scared, coming from someone with an artist's mentality, that hit home as a new year was birthed. I don't like mistakes; I don't like fear; but I also know comfort is a death trap of mediocrity.

There's a pendulum swing of wanting to continue taking risks while not screwing up. But the two can't exist without each other. I also know the screw-ups are the times when the most growth occurs. Dammit.

I reached back to the Beatitudes over those holidays. They're a supernatural reminder of how no real advancement can occur without a proper ass-kicking. Few, if any, of the Beatitudes can be lived out by winning while standing alone. We have to be leveled to understand those verses; they're simply too antithetical to our American, bootstrapped minds.

John Maisel of East-West Ministries said a line that's stuck with me since I heard him say it fifteen years ago. He was a captain in the Marine Corps in 1967 and awarded the Bronze Star and Purple Heart from his tour in Vietnam. I only met him a few times, but his genuine grace and humility penetrated to the core. He said, "You're either heading into a storm, are in the storm, or coming out of the storm. That's life on this side of heaven." Amen. I think that's why we struggle with coming out of the storm or moving into a new year. The calm waters and blue skies are brief before the seas of life begin churning again. If you're over forty, you know this is a fact because you can't hide from life anymore. It. Will. Get. You.

The other thing that stuck with me from the 2019 holidays was a prayer that a friend sent me by seventeenth-century philosopher Blaise Pascal, who I only know cuz he has a cool-ass lead singer name and because I read a great piece of theology by him years ago. This may be the greatest prayer I've ever read. As always, it seems like old dead guys say the best stuff. This one reeks of a posture of genuine grace. Why? Because he says, "I don't have the first clue as to what's best for me." Ain't a statement we hear often as we put on our hubris and our pride-filled pants.

> I ask of thee neither health, nor sickness, nor life, nor death; but that thou wilt dispose of my health and my sickness, my life and my death, for thy glory . . . Thou alone knowest what is most expedient for me; thou art the sovereign master, do what thou wilt. Give to me, take from me; but conform my will to thine . . . I know but one thing, that it is good to follow thee and that it is evil to offend thee. After this, I know not which is the better or worse of any thing; I know not which is more profitable to me, health or sickness, wealth or poverty, nor of all the things of the world. This is a discernment that exceeds the power of men or angels,

and that is hidden in the secrets of thy providence
which I adore, and which I wish not to fathom.[94]

This is a fear-inducing prayer—one we tepidly say, then walk back
with "But I don't *really* wanna be all in for what you think is best."
In other words, don't make it sting, and don't take my money,
home, and status.

I draw a level of comfort between the Gaiman and Pascal
quotes. Both come from a place of freedom, a groundedness that
understands we are not the center of the universe, navel-gazing be
damned. Gaiman is saying step out on the limb, and if it breaks,
who cares, because Pascal says you didn't know better, anyway.

Explore:

1) Have you given yourself to complete abandon of all circumstances, similar to Pascal's prayer?
2) Do you live your life making glorious, amazing mistakes,
or do you prefer to stay in your lane?

WEEK 48

23 MINUTES IN HELL

"I'm not afraid of dying. I just don't want to be there when it happens." [95]

—*Woody Allen*

There are different definitions of hell. Twenty-three minutes in rush hour traffic. Twenty-three minutes talking politics with the crazy uncle. Twenty-three minutes of the finale of *The Bachelorette*.

In his book *23 Minutes in Hell* and in an accompanying YouTube video, Bill Wiese describes his experience of a night in November of 1998 when he claims the Lord sent him down into the pit of hell for twenty-three minutes. Was I skeptical when I saw the YouTube link? Yep. Then I watched as he succinctly explained and quoted scripture to support his thesis. Being a Bible nerd, I cross-checked the verses he referenced to ensure he wasn't cherry-picking to create a best-selling narrative. His theology is accurate.

I often think fear is a shit deterrent; it pushes people away with a wave of a hand as opposed to leading with the inspiration and hope of God. I think it depends on the country and culture. When in Haiti or other third-world countries, hope is the olive branch that pulls people toward considering Christ. Here in affluenza-driven America, fear of a bad eternal destination seems apropos. I mention in *I'm Not Hitler* that trying to engage in a conversation about the possibility of hell, results in a whimsical concept of a dive bar with some shady characters, a lousy jukebox, and cheap whiskey. If only that were fact.

That's why Wiese's testimony resonates. He sounds lucid and fervent in his insistence that we need to be desperate in our desire to not end up there. The reality is that even if he's a complete nutcase, he is speaking about a subject all of us must consider. We know with 100% certainty we will leave this earth. As I've mentioned several times in my blogs and *I'm Not Hitler*, I'm astounded at our apathy toward the subject. Maybe I'm off in my assessment and the apathy is masking a deep fear of the unknown. Either way, we can't sit back and wait to go over the waterfall. We must address our individual end of life and grab a life preserver.

Where I jump on the Wiese train wholeheartedly is the accurate and controversial theology he unwraps in the video. It's a common refrain I hear: "I would never worship a God who sends people to hell." As Wiese says in agreement with mainstream theologians, pastors, and scholars, God doesn't send us. We choose it. "Uh, whuh you say!?" Listen to his analogies. Compelling.

Chew on this as a New Year's resolution. The logic works like this, and I delve much deeper in *I'm Not Hitler.*

- Start with the idea of intelligent design. There's overwhelming evidence of a theistic architect. Patterns and logic make up 90% of our world. The ordering of all things leans toward purpose, not randomness.

- Next, think of the idea of authority. Who has greater authority, you or God? (Surprisingly, this often stumps people.)
- Then ask, if God has the authority, does it seem logical that He usurps our opinions?
- Then question if there's a logical reason for God to be mean, evil, and contradictory.
- There appears to be evidence that He's loving, or at least benevolent at times. Yes, I recognize how tragedy in the world appears to say He is evil and mean, but there's another explanation available.
- Then ask this: if God is the ultimate loving authority, does it make sense that God would give us exact instructions for His creation to step into the next life? Or would He leave it up to us to create our own concepts? Remember, His authority is greater than ours.
- Would it make sense for Him to give one path to enter the next life? Or five, fifty, or 100 options that all contradict each other? Read what philosophers and logicians say about the law of contradiction, a crucial fact.
- Most importantly, look at the arc of your life. If there is a God who erases all past, present, and future mistakes, wouldn't that be worth exploring?

By far the toughest pill to swallow is why so many horrific things happen in this life, and God appears to be neutral about the outcomes. Scripture provides the best—albeit tough—answer in the form of an enemy who rules this side of heaven for a period of time. As 2 Corinthians 4:4 says, "The god of this age has blinded the minds of unbelievers, so that they cannot see the light of the gospel that displays the glory of Christ, who is the image of God."

This isn't foreign to us. We see a world filled with good guys and bad guys, whether it's in politics, film, or the opposing sports team. Think of Luke vs. Darth Vader, or pretty much every sci-fi film, or the bully on the playground. We're accustomed to good vs. evil throughout history.

This isn't to say God is powerless and under the authority of said enemy. To the contrary, for reasons a thousand times higher than our pay grade, He knows best when to intervene and when not to intervene. All the more reason to place our hope in a place devoid of pain and evil and follow the simple instructions for entry.

If you're rolling your eyes at the Wiese video and insistent that organized religion is a big crock, I agree with you on several fronts. We Jesus peeps are rife with hypocrisy. However, if you want to bet on the idea that you're gonna do your best to be a good person, live by the Golden Rule, and hope God agrees with your metrics, then please, *please*, PLEASE email me the conclusive list of good deeds. Confirm it with rigor and scholarly sources other than your zeal. Show me the definitive inventory God uses to measure our wholesome hearts, and include what happens when you don't live up to your standards. We all have our opinions, but I'm curious about "The List," the official index—or holy book—that rises above all others and deems Christ's efforts on the cross unnecessary.

While creating or searching for "The List," wrestle deeply with what Wiese says. It could be the most important thirty-four minutes you and your friends ever spend.

Explore:

1) Do you view scripture as an outdated, ancient rulebook designed to take the fun out of life?

2) Is the concept of hell real to you? Do you know any bad people who know they deserve to be in hell? (This question is somewhat sarcastic. I've never met anyone who thinks they deserve hell, yet so many of us believe we're good enough for entrance to heaven. Who exactly are the bad people who go to hell?)

WEEK 49

WHY I BELIEVE (PART 1 OF 3)

"Design is not just what it looks like and feels like. Design is how it works." [96]

—*Steve Jobs*

I understand the challenges of belief in a deity, particularly a loving God. Many of us come from dysfunctional families where the idea of a solid father figure is a distant laugh, so any mention of "God the Father" opens up scar tissue. Or we attended a church with a bunch of hypocritical wackadoos who turned us off like too much wasabi on sushi.

When I think back to my disbelief before my October 22nd, 1999 conversion, I realize my biggest impediment was pride. I was resolute in my belief that I could create my own definition of God, and he-she-it embodied everything I believed was cool and righteous, with an emphasis on cool. "My God likes the Rolling Stones, and wouldn't be caught dead with a Coors Light. No way he created cats—my God digs dogs. After all, what's 'God' spelled backwards?" Yep, I was a moron.

Before I delve into my personal journey, let's start with a foundational question: does God exist? In my experience, most folks who are not Jesus freaks land in an agnostic area. They believe there's something out there, but they're not crazy about organized religion. A common postmodern phrase is "I'm spiritual, not religious." Most of the time, those folks sound like I did in 1999, with a couple of sentences of Zen-like talk about nature and the universe serving as God, but they have no religious texts or prophets to speak of as ground zero for their foundation.

Atheists are a smaller percentage, often fervent in their stance that God is for simpletons and science is the answer to everything. We'll start there: intelligent design vs. evolution. The former states that there's some manner of architect (God) who created all things material and invisible, whether flesh, blood, dirt, air, water, minerals, biology, morality, love, sex, and all things in between. The latter says there is no engineer, and with only time plus a series of random events, all things came into being. An evolution thesis says there can't be any mention of agency or strategy, because that jumps over into the intelligent design camp, meaning some sort of brain was involved. The only variables are oodles of time plus lots of random events, like explosions and fire and lasers and such. Spoiler alert: name an explosion you know of that created order and not chaos. In other words, how many car explosions have you seen where a Volvo got all blow'd up and reassembled as a Ferrari . . . by itself?

Here's another way of looking at it. Wherever you are right now, you're surrounded by things that were intentionally designed. You're likely reading this post on a smartphone or computer that was *designed*. You're wearing a variety of clothes (hopefully) that were *designed*. You'll drive somewhere in a vehicle that was *designed*. You may be drinking a cup of coffee, and the cup was *designed*. You'll eat food throughout the day that follows an exact biological pattern to create the tomato, blueberry, or pork chop, and all were *designed*. You'll walk into a building that was meticulously *designed* by an architect and engineers. Got it? I can do this all day.

Even though everything I named was engineered by the most complex entity on the planet—humans—an evolutionist states that those same humans of staggering intellect were created by something that has no capacity for intellect. Meaning, evolution has no brain, yet somehow formed things that do have brains. No amount of time, not even hundreds of millions of years, could form any level of intelligence. A "choice" would have to be made to begin the assembly, and choice, strategy, pivoting, turning, starting, and stopping all require sequences of purpose, which requires intelligent design. You can't simply throw in another explosion— or a "singularity," as it's called in math and physics—and magically see patterns appear. Also, keep in mind, math and physics are never random.

When I was a new Christ follower, I had a myriad of questions specific to Him as God. However, one thing that utterly put the idea of atheism to bed was an illustration of a broken watch, a riff on eighteenth-century philosopher William Paley's position on natural theology. The thesis is this. Let's say I took a watch and busted it into a thousand pieces with a hammer, then placed all the pieces in a box and created a machine that began shaking the box. Whether shaking slow or fast, rhythmically or not, would the watch reform itself after millions of years? Of course not. There's no chance in hell. An evolutionist believes that with enough time, explosions, cosmic events, then more time . . . that's how our universe, and we peeps, came into existence.

For clarity, I do believe in evolution, but with an intelligent designer as the driver who uses it as a mechanism to execute His master plan for the universe. There are varying theological camps who don't believe in any level of evolution, but that's not the focus. The main point is there appears to be ironclad evidence of an intelligent designer of the highest order who created all things. We can call Him the great and powerful Oz, but that lends itself to charlatanry. Or we can call Him God.

The next questions: Can we know Him? Does He love us? Why does He allow pain?

Explore:

1) If you don't believe in God or organized religion, what are the issues that stop you from belief? Have you explored those hurdles in depth?

2) Are your challenges with religion more about the people, or is there an issue with God? Many people don't believe in God because of all the pain in the world. Is there an explanation for what appears to be malevolence?

WEEK 50

WHY I BELIEVE (PART 2 OF 3)

"Any fool can make a rule, and any fool will mind it." [97]

—*Henry David Thoreau*

I didn't birth me. I didn't will myself into being. I had nothing to do with my creation. My parents "did the deed," but they were also birthed through a process that was, at best, an activity. In other words, it's not like we humans have any level of democracy in how a child is formed. There ain't no hammers and nails or glue or spools of thread we use to create our little rugrats. All we offer is the sex, and presto—through a stunning miracle, a baby is formed. It's such a commonplace thing that we often forget how truly magical the birth of a human is. If we go back far enough, something birthed the first man and woman. A quick refresher: as stated in the previous chapter, the miracle can't start with science because science is not a thing-maker. Science is the study of the things, not the Creator and Designer. One definition of science is "a systematically organized body of knowledge on a particular subject." [98]

Science must have an intelligent designer using it as a tool, or it would be 100% impossible for it to be "a systematically organized body of knowledge." No brain, no system, no knowledge.

I recently watched the Netflix series *Inside Bill's Brain: Decoding Bill Gates*. His brain—like others in tech, medicine, or business—is astonishing in its processing power (he likens it to a CPU). But even Gates, like his parents and their parents before them, was birthed. He didn't have much to do with the horsepower given to that brain, and no level of parental encouragement or perfect schooling could fertilize such an intellect. A Creator determined and designed the fluency, capacity, and logic driving it. The same way Bill Gates and Steve Jobs created world changing computers, something created them.

The description above about science doesn't exactly create a feeling of joy. Personally, the words sound stifling and rigid. That's often how we view the Bible. One of the ageless questions of belief is this: can we know the God who created us? Christianity promises a relationship with the Creator of the Universe through belief in Jesus Christ. By believing in Him, we can have an actual relationship with God, the Creator of all things. There are several ways of saying and explaining it, but it's the idea that while God is still an entity of exponential proportions, through Christ and His sacrifice on the cross, we have access to a trinitarian God known as the Father, Son, and Holy Spirit. Because of Christ's actions, we can now talk with Him, rage at Him, seek wisdom from Him, and experience forgiveness in a way the most perfect parent or spouse could never understand or fulfill.

The Bible is the living, breathing document that helps us know the Trinity. "Uh, whuh?" Yes, scripture is not a rulebook; it's a living thing that speaks to us where we are in life's adventures when we're ten, twenty-five, forty-five, and seventy-five years old. Trust me, it's a fact, and it's the reason the inspired writing could only come from God. There's no reasonable explanation of how a book written over a 1,600-year timeline by upwards of thirty-nine different authors could still be relevant today, centuries after it came into existence. No level of human agency could be that prescient to weave together a document of this magnitude without divine penmanship. For example, why, how and for what purpose would John, in his Gospel, write this about Christ if it were not true?

> In the beginning was the Word, and the Word was with God, and the Word was God. He was with God in the beginning. Through him all things were made; without him nothing was made that has been made. In him was life, and that life was the light of all mankind.
>
> The Word became flesh and made his dwelling among us. We have seen his glory, the glory of the one and only Son, who came from the Father, full of grace and truth (John 1:1–4, 14).

Ah, yes, the grand conspiracy. That's one option. Let's dig into it a bit. Lots of folks think the Bible was created to control us malevolently, and the perpetrator was the church. If it was the church, the next logical question would be how did the church begin? Which will lead you back to the Bible, which includes the origin of the church. The origin of the church begins with God speaking to the Jewish people in the Old Testament and concludes with His Son, Jesus, fulfilling the prophecies of the Old Testament in the New Testament. In other words, the church had to begin somehow, and even secular historians consider the Old Testament and New Testament to pass assessments of veracity. So how does this conspiracy realistically manifest, and how have we been able to mask the cover-up for hundreds of years? Wouldn't there be a book of equal weight and historicity that could push back against biblical claims? I will bet bricks of cash that books by Dan Brown, Sam Harris, Richard Dawkins, and Christopher Hitchens won't be remembered even decades from now, let alone centuries. If you had to look them up, my point is already proven in their relevance versus Christ's. Plus, if I wander down the conspiracy trail and assume that the Bible is just a tool of control, the document doesn't read that way. It states over and over how a loving God has our best interest at heart and shows us a record of how He comes to the rescue over and over throughout history. In other words, the narrative doesn't read like a mean, restrictive government agency out to destroy mankind.

When I distill this three-part series down to a foundational debate, the issue is pride. I want to run my own life. I know what's best for me. I make my own rules. I don't need God to control me. The content in the Bible very much says that *we* want total management of our lives, and that we think we're smarter than the Being who created us.

This is why I push hard on folks to dive much deeper and not simply stop at "the Bible was written by humans, therefore I don't believe." That's a pride issue. Move past it. Why haven't seminaries and universities also stopped at that question? As I've said, every professor and scholar is well aware of the authorship, but they've chosen to spend their careers studying and teaching on the next level of questions. In other words, we don't disbelieve historical characters like George Washington, Napoleon, or Alexander the Great. We use historical data to evaluate their legitimacy. Therefore, let's do the same with Jesus Christ. Keep in mind, you won't find any viable organizations worshiping Washington,

Napoleon, or Alexander on Sunday mornings. Why is that? A large number of people around the world of different creeds, colors, and nationalities show up on Sundays, and all worship Jesus Christ. Not Abraham Lincoln, not Ghandi, not Nelson Mandela, not Shakespeare. Over two billion people claim allegiance to and look to one man as deity. That data must be measured and questioned against the other major faiths of Hinduism, Islam, Judaism, and Buddhism. Use scientific methodology if you want. Find empirical evidence to show that Christ followers are bonkers. Why do those folks believe, worship, and serve Him? Yep, could be a fear-based thing, where the massive conspiracy continues with mind control as the goal. Again, the narrative says Christ wants to give you, me, and everyone a more meaningful life on this side of heaven and eternal peace and happiness when we pass to the next. Christ made astonishing claims that force a decision. It's the classic C. S. Lewis mind twister of three options: Christ is either a liar, a lunatic, or exactly who He claimed and proved. He's the one true Son of God, the Creator of the universe, and our Lord and Savior. Wrestle with the options.

Scripture also gives us the foundation for right and wrong. I regularly have discussions on how mankind can discern morality when it comes to truth. It's a significant part of the thesis of my first book. Every Friday morning, I sit with a group of good friends who discuss the idea. Some in the group believe the only way to discern right and wrong is to look to the Creator as the source, meaning that God is the arbitrator of truth and morality. If that's a fact, then we must answer the question of did God speak through the Torah, the Quran, the Bible, or some other document? Others in the group are adamant that people decide what's right and wrong, and they use documents like the Constitution as the final authority. It's interesting how there is belief in a man-made document like the Constitution, but disbelief in another document also written by people (the Bible) that's been tested, questioned, and studied ten times more than the Constitution. The secular worldview says that people have final authority and agency; in other words, we're the top of the totem pole, so we make the decisions, thereby stripping God of His jurisdiction. A theological worldview says that only God has absolute authority, since created thing (people) cannot usurp the Creator.

This is where I get practical in *I'm Not Hitler*. As an artist, the canvas doesn't have dominion over me, the creator. I choose the paint, colors, composition, and overall meaning of the piece. The canvas can only receive what I choose to give it. The canvas has no agency; I'm the creator. Or, at a company, there's a CEO. He or she has final authority of the organization. We can only follow the rules of the person, team, or board who created the entity. Yes, we can quit a job, but that doesn't give us authority over one boss or the next. The challenge when taking God out of the picture is the age-old conundrum of how can one person or a thousand people know who is the most right when discerning truth? We know from our democracy that individuals and groups can never agree. This leads to another interesting data point. When a person has connected with or surrendered to God, the question of authority is clear-cut; there's no discussion. It's like questioning whether air exists. Of course God knows best. God created everything in the universe. It doesn't follow logic that the Creator of all things would then reduce Himself to a smaller position of dominion underneath "things" to which He gave birth. In simplistic terms, it's like a four-year-old running a household with the parents taking orders from the child.

Explore:

1) Are you comfortable with the idea of God as our Creator, but challenged by the idea of Him speaking through men and women in the Bible? Explore why.

2) Why do you think many people struggle with God as the final authority? Does pride have an influence?

WEEK 51

WHY I BELIEVE—MY CONVERSION (PART 3 OF 3)

"All I have seen teaches me to trust the Creator for all I have not seen." [99]

—*Ralph Waldo Emerson*

Twenty years ago, I went on a journey—a five-day fast in the New Mexico desert, with my only sustenance a bag of peyote to expand my mind to an altered dimension. On day two at 3 a.m., the Shaman above appeared from behind—I kid you not—a glowing boulder. At first, I thought it was a hallucinatory dream. When he spoke, I entered into a trance-like fog, where in a whispery chant, he told me he was the incarnation of Jesus Christ. And voilà, in the mystical hills of Santa Fe, I transformed into a Jesus zombie.

If only that were true.

Before I became a Christ follower, I thought the whole religion thing was some fanatical crutch for weak people. Come on . . .

burning bushes, seas parting, a dude living in a whale? If the religious folk I met were hardcore about it, I thought they were narrow-minded zealots. Or, if they were all smiley and sugary, I figured maybe they had smoked some weed to induce their fantasy for the make-believe. As I mentioned in *I'm Not Hitler*, I vividly recall thinking, *I want nothing to do with that nonsense. Fer freak's sake, they listen to Amy Grant, wear dopey clothes, and hate gay people. What a bunch of morons!* My ignorance had nothing to do with who Christ is and what He desires for us. I figured the Bible was all man-made baloney.

Then, on Friday, October 22nd, 1999 around 8 p.m., everything changed. I was sitting in my car with a gal I had dated, and we were discussing whether we should rethink our status. There wasn't any hanky-panky. No kissing. No big, bawling emotions. Only a conversation. I said, "Wendy (changed her name here), I'm wondering if we made a mistake. Maybe we should go out again." My right hand was on the middle console, and she put her left hand on mine and said nonchalantly, "Don't worry. It's going to be all right." For real this time—I kid you not—I had a feeling similar to my funny bone being zinged. We finished our conversation, had a quick hug, and then she went to her car and I headed home. I still remember how crystal clear the night felt as I drove down Swiss Avenue toward my Deep Ellum hood. I had this strange sense of peace and warmth. I remember thinking, *Am I in love with her? No, this is different—has nothing to do with her.*

For the next two to three days, the author C. S. Lewis was on my mind. The way I describe it is similar to how you have a craving for pizza or sushi; he kept popping up in my head throughout the day. I remember thinking, *He was the atheist dude who became a Christian . . . I think?* Not having a clue how the Holy Spirit provides those intuitions, I reached out to a good friend, David, a born-again Jesus freak, and asked if he knew anything about Lewis. He did, and sent me *Mere Christianity*, Lewis's landmark apologetic discourse. To say it leveled me like a grenade doesn't do it justice. As I read the book over the next month, the words leapt off the page and pummeled me. I remember saying out loud through tears of undeniable joy, "Oh. My. God. This Christian shit is real!" This wasn't a flight of fancy. It was ground zero, and twenty years later, I lead multiple Bible studies, have been on eighteen mission trips, and spend each and every day with that Christ dude on the forefront of damn near every thought. I've met Africans, Indians, Salvadorians, and Haitians with stories that mirror mine: they encountered Christ and got taken to their knees.

Yep, if I were you, I'd say the same thing I used to say to my Jesus freak friends: "Good for you, pal, but I'm not interested." Ah, but this is where it gets good. HE'S INTERESTED IN YOU. What do most of us want? Nope, not fame, money, sex, or vacations. Yes, those things are damn nice, amen. But deep down, in those places in our hearts that scare us, we want relief. We want peace, comfort, and rest; the deep sigh of knowing things will be okay. We want respite from the anxiety, worry, and disappointment of life, or the low-level anger of dreams that didn't pan out. The grace of Jesus Christ offers those things, plus forgiveness of all past, present, and future mistakes.

> Come to me, all you who are weary and burdened, and I will give you rest. Take my yoke upon you and learn from me, for I am gentle and humble in heart, and you will find rest for your souls. For my yoke is easy and my burden is light (Matthew 11:28–30).

If that's real, if He is an elixir that can keep you from drowning when life kicks—and it *will* kick—then why not give it a shot? Keep the Netflix, keep hard-charging on the career, stick with the meditation, crush it in CrossFit, but add a big dose of Christ too. Challenge God to reveal Himself to you. Here's the prayer at the end of *I'm Not Hitler.* Say something similar for a couple of weeks every day and keep your radar up for unusual signals and intuitions.

> God, if you're real, I want to know You. I'm not sure what I believe about You or heaven or the idea that I'm not good enough for entrance. Show me the path. If this Jesus guy is relevant, if He's real, if He can help me and make my life better, I'm all ears. Right now, I think it's all horseshit, but I want to know truth. Show me the way. I've heard the word "grace" before, but it means nothing to me now. Help me understand. Amen.

As I said in the previous chapter, I encourage you to move past the fact that the Bible was written by people. Please hear me: I'm not saying dismiss the reality. I'm challenging you to ask tougher questions. For example, today I went to lunch with an attorney friend who's interested in learning more about Christ. I told her to read the four Gospels, and to keep in mind that the reason there are four is that they give multiple accounts of Christ for different audiences and purposes. Matthew is for a Jewish audience, focusing on Christ as the ultimate rabbi. Mark is succinct and Hemingway-esque and focuses on God's immediacy via miracles. Luke was a physician and writes with more detail, and as the only non-Jewish Gospel writer, targets a Gentile audience. John's Gospel, the only non-Synoptic book, helps explain the character and love of Christ. Even with her big ol' brain, she wasn't aware of that short list of differences in those four books. I encouraged her to focus on the red words, as those are Christ speaking. I ask the same of anyone reading this who doesn't fully understand why this guy is so special. You don't have to be open-minded; you can walk in the door calling bullshit on the whole thing. If Christ and scripture can't withstand all your questions and doubts, it's a house of cards anyway, right?

Regarding the context of the Bible, keep in mind that it's not written as a documented history of the world with explanations of physics, dinosaurs, and the rings of Saturn. You don't have to separate science and faith, but do know it's not a scientific book. It's a record of how God has chased mankind through the centuries and how He desperately wants a relationship with every single one of us. In other words, it's an extended love letter showing the extravagant methods God initiated to fix a broken relationship.

Yes, compare the major religions. Start with the Abrahamic faiths of Judaism, Islam, and Christianity. Go Eastern with Buddhism and Hinduism. Are they all the same? Can five contradictory doctrines all be true?

Please do compare atheist books *The God Delusion* by Richard Dawkins, *God Is Not Great: How Religion Poisons Everything* by Christopher Hitchens, and *The End of Faith* by Sam Harris. The authors are adamant in their positions that they've disproved Christ and the Bible and that belief in God has hurt mankind. Their thesis is this: you and I are a cosmic accident. You have thirty to ninety years, give or take, and then you become dust; there is no anything after death. You don't RIP, you simply end and become nothingness. If that's true, you better get your shit together fast, because the clock is ticking and "nothing" is coming your way. If you were urgent before, you better giddyup, because you only have maybe fifteen to twenty years of prime living before physical decline begins. If you want to bet on an atheist doctrine, don't pray, don't cry out for something larger in your soul to provide solace, MAKE THAT BUCKET LIST HAPPEN . . . tick-tock-tick-tock. Figure out life on your own because it's all us, baby, and no second act, no heaven. This is as good as it gets. And scene.

If you prefer being "spiritual and not religious" and you don't need Christ's love and forgiveness, make sure you've passed the test for being good enough for heavenly entrance. I don't know of any test, but I hear non-Jesus folks say they've been good people, so I assume they know the cutoff point between the good people and the bad people. I assume there's some sort of accurate measure they're aware of that I've never been able to locate. I'm just not sure that trying to do my best to live by the Golden Rule is how God operates. I suggest you ask Him, since He seems to be top of the totem pole. Keep in mind that if you kick Christ to the curb, your "spiritual" belief has to withstand the same rigorous questions we throw at the Bible. In other words, is it authoritative? Will we wear necklaces in your honor? Will your thesis be discussed centuries from now?

Here's the piece that sounds all woo-woo. The words "born again" have been bastardized in our culture, the same with saying Jesus died for your sins. What does that even mean? Hell, even I struggle with the definition, and I'm full-on crazy about the dude. We believers often mention "heart change," and it's difficult to articulate. The best I can say is that your vision changes from astigmatism to, like, 3D steroid super goggles. Your life expands exponentially in terms of depth, hope, inspiration, and understanding of pain. Don't get me wrong—believing in Christ doesn't ensure a white picket fence and no more struggle. Far from it; the challenges remain, but with a new temperament and purpose to help you navigate the ups and downs. For years after my conversion, I had a feeling of "fullness." That's the best way I can explain it. It was like a hole I didn't know existed had became exquisitely paved. As I write these words now, I can feel the weight of the fullness. It's a recognition of something infinitely larger than me that now permeates my thoughts and feelings. Yes, it *IS* magic, it *IS* supernatural, and He *IS* miraculous. When the connection happens, you'll know it, same as you know you have air in your lungs.

Explore:

1) Have you had a dramatic, life-altering event that you describe as supernatural? Did it affect your spiritual life?

2) Are you hesitant to explore Christ, afraid your life will narrow if you believe in Him? Take all the worries and concerns to Him in prayer and see if your perceptions were the narrow piece of the equation.

WEEK 52

WAS THAT RANDOM?

*"From where we stand the rain seems random. If we could
stand somewhere else, we would see the order in it."* [100]

—*Tony Hillerman,* Coyote Waits

I like the words "touch point." I use them to describe times
in my life when a mammoth-sized, invisible index finger drops
out of heaven and thumps me on the noggin. I've got a jour-
nal somewhere that has the major ones I can recall. They're
the things that change the course of your life—maybe the day
you met your spouse, or a phone call from the doctor that you
didn't expect. The touch points are not always pleasant. Possibly,
maybe, a dear friend of mine just had one of those moments. I'm
convinced he did.

In the previous chapter, I suggested that folks who don't sub-
scribe to that dude on the cross should try a little prayer, essentially
a brass-tacks theological bet for God to reveal Himself. One of
my closest friends took me up on the wager. He and I had been

discussing my first book over a beer at The Old Monk, a local pub, and he had several of the big questions that make all of us shake our heads in disbelief about God. For several nights in a row after the Monk, he said the prayer, and the next Sunday morning he texted me this:

> So I've been giving a little 'shout out' . . . as you had mentioned in your book, every day since we had our chat at the Monk . . . so this morning I was having coffee with my mother at Merit Coffee . . . we left, and a nice, young guy came running out asking us to wait. I thought I had left my phone or something. He wanted to know if he could have a quick word with me, I said sure. He said he had this strong feeling about me and that he felt I was filled with questions and was searching for something and he wanted me to be open to allowing Christ in my life . . . I thought I was being punked!! I seriously was looking around for where you were . . . (you weren't punking me, were you?) . . . then he said God Bless you and walked back to Merit . . . wow.

Shazam! I kinda dig it when God responds in such a literal way. Or did He? That's the question for all of us. As much as we want God to appear in a puff of harp-filled smoke or float down out of heaven like Superman and speak directly to us, He seems to prefer leaving it up to us to discern whether divine intervention took place. Or did some random dude decide on his own, on that particular morning, to approach my friend, a stranger to him, and mention Jesus Christ? Things that make you go hmmmm.

The question for all non-Christian folks is whether this encounter is only for a select few. In other words, can you say, "Good for you, buddy, but I'm not interested. Life is good as is?" Sure you can; you have free will to do anything you prefer, and we often do. However, you can't escape the exit that's coming for all of us. You're gonna check out of this hotel at some point, and Jesus may be *the* concierge steering us to the next one.

Let's circle back to touch points and give some thought to yours. For me, there are a few "bigguns" that come to mind. One changed the course of my life with work, and it was roughly ten years before I became a Jesus freak. I was twenty-three years old, had recently graduated college, and was having cold feet about moving to Los Angeles. I was at a local bar watching blues musician Albert Collins and wearing a jean jacket with an image of Stevie Ray Vaughan on the back that I had painted by hand. As I stood there listening to the music, I felt someone behind me grabbing the bottom of the jacket to stretch it out. I turned around and saw this ultra-cool gal with brilliant dreadlocks. She asked, "Where'd you get that jacket!?" I said, "I painted it." Her mouth fell open and she spun me around to look again, then whirled me back to face her. "YOU painted this!?" "Yes," I said. She handed me her business card and said, "We'll buy these from you." I looked on the card and saw that she worked for Warner Bros. I remember blinking at her and stammering like Keanu Reeves, "Whuhhhh?"

That changed everything for me and began my art career, which led to me being an entrepreneur. Second only to my Christ encounter, that was the biggest touch point in my life. I have a choice. I can look at that circumstance and see it as one of hundreds of innocuous forks in the road with no relevance other than a direction to take. Or . . . did God give me a nudge then, same as He did again when I was thirty-two? Has He been moving chess pieces to create a path from birth? A series of questions have to be answered. Is there a God? Is it-she-he knowable? Is God sovereign or only a timekeeper? Does God care about His creation? Somewhere in the five, ten, or fifty questions, the Bible and Christ have to be considered. Why? Because the two entities have more weight than any other book, king, or president in the history of the world. No, you cannot dismiss the questions and be apathetic. Why? Because you have an expiration date, and making an assumption that you'll be fine answers one of those fifty questions about who has the final authority. Here's a hint: it ain't you.

On a smaller scale, but equally important, was a time—after becoming a Jesus freak—when I was dead-ass broke and waiting on a small check from a client. I was in dire straits and had sold my CDs and a guitar to scrape up some coins, and had even given blood for some extra scratch. On that particular day, my gas tank was on E, and on my way home I said an anxiety-filled prayer: "God, I need some help here." Twenty minutes later, I pulled up to the gate at my studio, opened the car door to punch in the code, and with my first step out of the car, saw a $20 bill on the ground. I had a choice to think, *Gee, how random*, but instead, I held it up to the sky, shook my head, and said, "Thank you."

I'm reluctant to say "God has a plan" because people have abused it in vacuous ways during the most inopportune moments. But He does. He is getting the attention of my friend I mentioned earlier, and it seems damn near tomfoolery to guess otherwise. If you don't know Christ, say the prayer and ask Him to be real. Then keep your radar up for how He woos you into a relationship. None of it is chance; every item was ordered specifically for you.

Explore:

1) In your life, have you experienced circumstances or events you knew couldn't be random?

2) Think of the barriers keeping you from trusting that God has a specific, meaningful plan for your life. Pray about your doubts and ask the Lord to help you believe in His masterful navigation.

IN CLOSING

What's next? Try the prayer I mentioned in week 51. Here it is again. Try your own version of it for several days in a row. Pay attention to any "random" events, maybe a friend asking for a prayer, could be an article that comes across your newsfeed. When you knock on the door of God, He will respond. Might not be as fast as a microwave, but the heat will come if you bang consistently.

> God, if you're real, I want to know You. I'm not sure what I believe about You or heaven or the idea that I'm not good enough for entrance. Show me the path. If this Jesus guy is relevant, if He's real, if He can help me and make my life better, I'm all ears. Right now, I think it's all horseshit, but I want to know truth. Show me the way. I've heard the word "grace" before, but it means nothing to me now. Help me understand. Amen.

Please reach out with questions. I'd love to continue this conversation and do my best to answer your questions.

Thank you for taking time to read my words. I'm honored.

Warmest regards,
Mike Lyon
Mike@artisticlyon.com

ACKNOWLEDGMENTS

To amazing friends and strangers who encourage my writing. To all the 28:1 guys, Friday morning Diversity of Thought mix of men, and the Saturday morning Blood Brothers. Thank you for keeping me on my toes, and leaning into the Lord.

To my amazing proofreader and editor, Meaghan Minkus, for being sharp, funny and over the top professional.

Of course big thanks to my mom, for your unending support and love of our family.

NOTES

1. *Anthony Bourdain: Parts Unknown*, season 4, episode 1, "Shanghai," directed by Nick Brigden, written by Anthony Bourdain, featuring Anthony Bourdain, aired September 28, 2014, on CNN.
2. "Five Common Misconceptions About Trauma," Psychology Today, October 27, 2015, https://www.psychologytoday.com/us/blog/turning-straw-gold/201510/five-common-misconceptions-about-trauma.
3. John Calvin, *Institutes of the Christian Religion*, Book 1, Chapter 2, Part 1, https://www.ccel.org/ccel/calvin/institutes.iv.iii.html.
4. Tim Keller, "David and Bathsheba," August 23, 2009 https://gospelinlife.com/downloads/david-and-bathsheba-6017/).
5. Max Marshall, "Growing Up with Steve Miller," *Texas Monthly*, June 2018, https://www.texasmonthly.com/articles/young-musician-growing-up-with-steve-miller/.
6. Mehmet Murat Ildan Quotations, September 12, 2020 https://muratildanquotations.wordpress.com/

7. Nathaniel Penn, "The Curious Cons of the Man Who Wouldn't Die," *GQ*, May 20, 2019, https://www.gq.com/story/the-man-who-wouldnt-die.

8. Elizabeth Gilbert, *Eat, Pray, Love* (London: Bloomsbury Publishing, 2006), 165.

9. 444 Parl. Deb. H.C. (5th ser.) (1947) cols. 206–207.

10. Oswald Chambers, *My Utmost for His Highest* (Grand Rapids: Discovery House, 1992), 150.

11. Ray Wylie Hubbard, vocalist, "Conversation with the Devil," by Ray Wylie Hubbard, track4 on *Crusades of the Restless Knights*, Philo, 1999.

12. *The Black Godfather*, aired June 7, 2019, on Netflix .

13. Apple, "The Crazy Ones," advertisement aired on September 28, 1997, one minute.

14. John Steinbeck, *East of Eden* (New York: Penguin, 1952), 301.

15. "Moxie," Urban Dictionary, updated December 21, 2006, https://www.urbandictionary.com/define.php?term=Moxie.

16. "Fortitude," American Heritage® Dictionary of the English Language, Fifth Edition, 2016 by Houghton Mifflin Harcourt Publishing Company.

17. Albert Camus, *The Rebel*, trans. Anthony Bower (New York: Knopf Doubleday Publishing Group, 2012), 104.

18. *Ugly Delicious*, season 1, episode 1, "Pizza," directed by Eddie Schmidt, featuring David Chang, Aziz Ansari, et. al., aired February 23, 2018, on Netflix.

19. Tupac Shakur, *MTV News*, MTV, August 21, 1992, http://www.mtv.com/news/2870384/tupac-calls-out-trumps-greed-in-this-unseen-1992-mtv-interview/.

20. Richelle E. Goodrich, *Slaying Dragons* (self-pub., CreateSpace Independent Publishing Platform, 2017).

21. J. K. Rowling, *Harry Potter and the Sorcerer's Stone* (New York: Scholastic Press, 1998), 298.

22. "American Are Most Likely to Base Truth on Feelings," *Barna*, February 12, 2002 https://www.barna.com/research/americans-are-most-likely-to-base-truth-on-feelings/.
23. Ibid.
24. "Truth—Satyam, a Talk" by Pravrajika Sevaprana, November 18, 2018 https://vedanta.org/2019/general-news/truth-satyam-a-talk-by-pravrajika-sevaprana.
25. History.com editors, "Rwandan Genocide," *History*, last updated September 30, 2019, https://www.history.com/topics/africa/rwandan-genocide.
26. Aldous Huxley, *Proper Studies* (London: Chatto and Windus, 1929).
27. "True north," Wikipedia, Wikipedia Foundation, Inc., last updated May 3, 2020, https://en.wikipedia.org/wiki/True_north.
28. "The Declaration of Independence: What Does It Say?", The U.S. National Archives and Records Administration, last updated December 14, 2018, https://www.archives.gov/founding-docs/declaration/what-does-it-say.
29. John Fea, "Religion and Early Politics: Benjamin Franklin and His Religious Beliefs," *Pennsylvania Heritage*, vol. 37, no. 4, Fall 2011, http://www.phmc.state.pa.us/portal/communities/pa-heritage/religion-early-politics-benjamin-franklin.html.
30. *The Usual Suspects*, directed by Bryan Singer (Universal City, California; PolyGram Films, 1995), 1 hr. 46 min.
31. Milliken v. Bradley, 418 U.S. 717 at 165 (1974).
32. Jonathan Pokluda, "The Greatest Sin," June 4, 2020, https://www.harriscreek.org/the-greatest-sin/
33. Anton LaVey, *The Satanic Bible*, (New York: Avon Books, 1969).
34. Sylvia Plath, *The Bell Jar* ([Portsmouth]: Heinemann, 1963), 24.

35. Chuck Klosterman, "Kobe Bryant Will Always Be an All-Star of Talking," *GQ*, February 18, 2015, https://www.gq.com/story/kobe-bryant-nba-allstar.

36. Lesslie Newbigin, *Foolishness to the Greeks: The Gospel and Western Culture* (Grand Rapids, MI: Wm. B. Eerdmans Publishing Company, 1986).

37. Louise Glück, *Descending Figure* (New York: Ecco Press, 1980).

38. David Brooks, "Do You Have to Be a Jerk to Be Great?", *The New York Times*, July 29, 2019, https://www.nytimes.com/2019/07/29/opinion/work-relationships.html.

39. Ibid.

40. Ibid.

41. Michael Buckley, *The Fairy-Tale Detectives* (New York: Amulet Books, 2005), 18.

42. Heidi Maibom, "Spot the Psychopath," *Aeon*, August 6, 2019, https://aeon.co/essays/you-have-more-in-common-with-a-psychopath-than-you-realise.

43. Ibid.

44. Yohji Yamamoto, "Yohji Yamamoto x Gata Magazine: 'Vanishing Vision,'" 2020, https://gatamagazine.com/articles/fashion/yohji-yamamoto-gata-magazine-vanishing-vision.

45. John Eldredge, *Beautiful Outlaw: Experiencing the Playful, Disruptive, Extravagant Personality of Jesus* (Nashville, TN: FaithWords, 2011), 137.

46. John F. Kennedy, "Commencement Address" (speech), Yale University, June 11, 1962, New Haven, CT, transcript and mp4 audio, 30:38, https://www.jfklibrary.org/about-us/about-the-jfk-library/kennedy-library-fast-facts/rededication-film-quote.

47. Anne Lamott, *Bird by Bird: Some Instructions on Writing and Life* (New York: Anchor Books, 1995), 22.

48. Anne Lamott, *Traveling Mercies: Some Thoughts on Faith* (New York: Anchor Books, 1999), 82.

49. *American Factory*, directed by Steven Bognar and Julia Reichert (Los Angeles, CA: Higher Ground Productions, 2019), 1 hr. 55 min.

50. Ibid.

51. Jon Bloom, "Why You Have That Thorn," *Desiring God*, April 13, 2018, https://www.desiringgod.org/articles/why-you-have-that-thorn.

52. David L. Wolfe, *Epistemology: The Justification of Belief* (Downers Grove, IL: InterVarsity Press, 1982), 69.

53. Rex Huppke, "Column: Bret Stephens, Donald Trump and the Epidemic of Male Fragility," *Chicago Tribune*, August 28, 2019, https://www.chicagotribune.com/columns/rex-huppke/ct-bret-stephens-bedbug-trump-warren-male-fragility-huppke-20190828-bym26nfh3vgfreze7zpvqymdzm-story.html.

54. Apollon Maykov, untitled poem, dated 1878.

55. Elizabeth Gilbert, "Elizabeth Gilbert Shows Up for . . . Everything," interview by Chris Anderson, *The TED Interview*, TED Conferences LLC, October 19, 2018, transcript and audio, 58:57, https://www.ted.com/talks/the_ted_interview_elizabeth_gilbert_shows_up_for_everything/transcript?language=en.

56. Elizabeth Gilbert (@elizabeth_gilbert_writer), "Dear Ones: This picture of me and Rayya was taken one year ago today . . .", Instagram photo, June 6, 2018, https://www.instagram.com/p/Bjr8FFTDS3j/.

57. James Baldwin, "Telling Talk from a Negro Writer," interview by Jane Howard, *LIFE*, vol. 54, no. 21 (May 24, 1963): 89.

58. Criss Jami, *Diotima, Battery, Electric Personality* (self-pub., CreateSpace Independent Publishing Platform, 2013).

59. *Merriam-Webster*, s.v. "cowardice" (*n.*), accessed September 24, 2020, https://www.merriam-webster.com/dictionary/cowardice.

60. Dave Miller, Ph.D., "Hematidrosis: Did Jesus Sweat Blood?", Apologetics Press, Inc., 2004, https://apologeticspress.org/apcontent.aspx?category=11&article=1086.

61. *Theater of Life*, aired on October 10, 2016 on Netflix, https://www.imdb.com/title/tt5331878/.

62. "The Status of Hunger in North Texas," North Texas Food Bank, September 25, 2019, https://ntfb.org/the-status-of-hunger-in-north-texas/.

63. Blog "The Status of Hunger in North Texas," September 25, 2019, https://ntfb.org/the-status-of-hunger-in-north-texas.

64. C. S. Lewis, *Mere Christianity* (San Francisco: HarperSan Francisco, Harper edition, 2001), 134.

65. Ibid.

66. Anne Lamott, *Traveling Mercies: Some Thoughts on Faith* (New York: Anchor Books, 1999), 134.

67. Malcolm Gladwell, *The Tipping Point: How Little Things Can Make a Big Difference* (New York: Little, Brown, 2006), 259.

68. Bill Bryson, *A Short History of Nearly Everything* (New York: Broadway Books, 2003), 122.

69. Carey Scott, "Oh friend . . . I know you are exhausted from the battle . . . ", Facebook, October 24, 2019, https://www.facebook.com/careyscotttalks/posts/oh-friendi-know-you-are-exhausted-from-the-battlei-know-youre-afraid-things-will/2828865360466685/.

70. Victoria Dsouza, "100+ Pablo Picasso Quotes From The Profound Spanish Artist," June 17, 2019, https://comicbookandbeyond.com/pablo-picasso-quotes.

71. Daniel Bukszpan, "Dave Chappelle's Netflix Special Is Offending Critics, but Viewers Don't Care," CNBC, September 7, 2019, https://www.cnbc.com/2019/09/07/dave-chappelles-netflix-special-is-offending-critics-but-viewers-dont-care.html.

72. Kanye West, "Airpool Karaoke," interview with James Corden, *The Late Late Show with James Corden*, CBS, October 28, 2019, https://www.cbs.com/shows/late-late-show/video/euLnFzxc Vlo9rivOGJ6qq1fChLLzxJYD/kanye-west-airpool-karaoke/.

73. Billy Graham, "Answers," 2019. https://www.billygraham.ca/answer/can-you-give-me-even-one-reason-to-give-my-life-to-jesus/

74. Gary Brandenburg, "A Crash Course on Happiness," November 3, 2019, sermon, Fellowship Dallas, Dallas, TX, mp4 video, 44:51, https://subsplash.com/fellowshipdallas/media/mi/+mms6h9v.

75. Jeff Warren, Twitter, November 8, 2019, @Jeff_Warren

76. Dan Pearce, *Single Dad Laughing,* (Independently published, 2011).

77. Michael Pratt, (Officer, U.S. Army, West Point –The U.S. Military Academy), in discussion with the author, November 17, 2019.

78. Christine Caine, "Before you chase after success, know what success is," Facebook, January 12, 2020, https://www.facebook.com/theChristineCaine/photos/a.10150570623045089/10163026264635089/?type=3.

79. Andy Crouch, "It's Time to Reckon with Celebrity Power," The Gospel Coalition, March 24, 2018, https://www.thegospelcoalition.org/article/time-reckon-celebrity-power/.

80. John Eldredge, *Waking the Dead: The Glory of a Heart Fully Alive* (Nashville, TN: Thomas Nelson, 2003), 58.

81. Jeanne Marie Laskas, "The Mister Rogers No One Saw," *The New York Times Magazine*, November 19, 2019, https://www.nytimes.com/2019/11/19/magazine/mr-rogers.html.

82. *Merriam-Webster*, s.v. "saint (*n.*)," accessed September 25, 2020, https://www.merriam-webster.com/dictionary/saint.

83. Tom Junod, "Can You Say . . . Hero?", *Esquire*, November 1, 1998, https://classic.esquire.com/article/1998/11/1/can-you-say-hero.

84. Mokokoma Mokhonoana, books and essays, 2020, https://mokokoma.com/.

85. "Black Friday Statistics 2019," Finder, updated November 6, 2019, https://www.finder.com/black-friday-statistics.

86. "Giving Tuesday Statistics for Nonprofits," Nonprofits Source, accessed September 25, 2020, https://nonprofits-source.com/online-giving-statistics/giving-tuesday/.

87. Henry Winkler, "Not My Job: We Quiz Actor Henry Winkler on Twinklers," interview by Peter Sagal, *Wait Wait . . . Don't Tell Me!*, NPR, August 10, 2019, https://www.npr.org/2019/08/10/749692259/not-my-job-we-quiz-actor-henry-winkler-on-twinklers.

88. Neil Mccormick, "Lady GaGa: Pop Meets Art to Just Dance," *The Telegraph*, January 21, 2009, https://www.telegraph.co.uk/culture/4307251/Lady-GaGa-pop-meets-art-to-just-dance.html.

89. Sarah Lyall, "George Harrison Stabbed in Chest by an Intruder," *The New York Times*, December 31, 1999, https://www.nytimes.com/1999/12/31/world/george-harrison-stabbed-in-chest-by-an-intruder.html.

90. J. Maureen Henderson, "One in Four Millennials Would Quit Their Job to Be Famous," *Forbes*, January 24, 2017, https://www.forbes.com/sites/jmaureenhenderson/2017/01/24/

one-in-four-millennials-would-quit-their-job-to-be-famous/#49117532c438.

91. Maya Angelou, *Wouldn't Take Nothing for My Journey Now* (New York: Random House, 1993), 138.

92. Salvador Dalí, *The Secret Life of Salvador Dalí*, trans. Haakon Chevalier (New York: Dover Publications, 1993), 1.

93. Journal.NeilGaiman.com (blog); "My New Year Wish," by Neil Gaiman, posted December 31, 2011.

94. Blaise Pascal, *The Harvard Classics vol. 48: Blaise Pascal: Thoughts, Letters, and Minor Works*, ed. Charles W. Eliot, trans. W. F. Trotter, M. L. Booth, and O. W. Wright (New York: P. F. Collier & Son, 1910), 372–3.

95. Woody Allen, *Without Feathers* (New York: Random House Publishing Group, 1972), 106.

96. Rob Walker, "The Guts of a New Machine," *The New York Times Magazine,* November 30, 2003, https://www.nytimes.com/2003/11/30/magazine/the-guts-of-a-new-machine.html.

97. Henry David Thoreau, Main article: "Civil Disobedience," September 26, 1859.

98. *Lexico,* s.v. "science (*n.*)," accessed September 25, 2020, https://www.lexico.com/en/definition/science.

99. Ralph Waldo Emerson, *Self-Reliance*, First Series, 1847.

100. Tony Hillerman, Coyote Waits, (New York: Harper & Row, 1990), 214.

Made in the USA
Monee, IL
26 June 2022

98636083R00144